Campaign Against Racism an

SOUTHALL

THE BIRTH OF A BLACK COMMUNITY

Published by the Institute of Race Relations
and Southall Rights

ISBN 0 85001 0225

The Campaign Against Racism and Fascism (CARF) grew out of the All London Anti-racist Anti-fascist Co-ordinating Committee. It published the paper *CARF* from 1977-1979; since then it has provided a regular anti-racist section to the magazine *Searchlight*. CARF is based at the Institute of Race Relations.

Southall Rights is a free local advice centre formed in 1976 after the murder of Gurdip Singh Chaggar. It defended many of those arrested on April 23, 1979. Since April 1981 it has had law centre status. It is located at 54 High Street, Southall.

Typeset by Lithoprint, 329 Upper Street, London N1
Cover design By M
Cover photo by G. Cookson, *Socialist Challenge*
Printed by the Russell Press, Gamble Street, Nottingham
Distributed by the Institute of Race Relations, 247 Pentonville Road, London N1 9NG

Contents

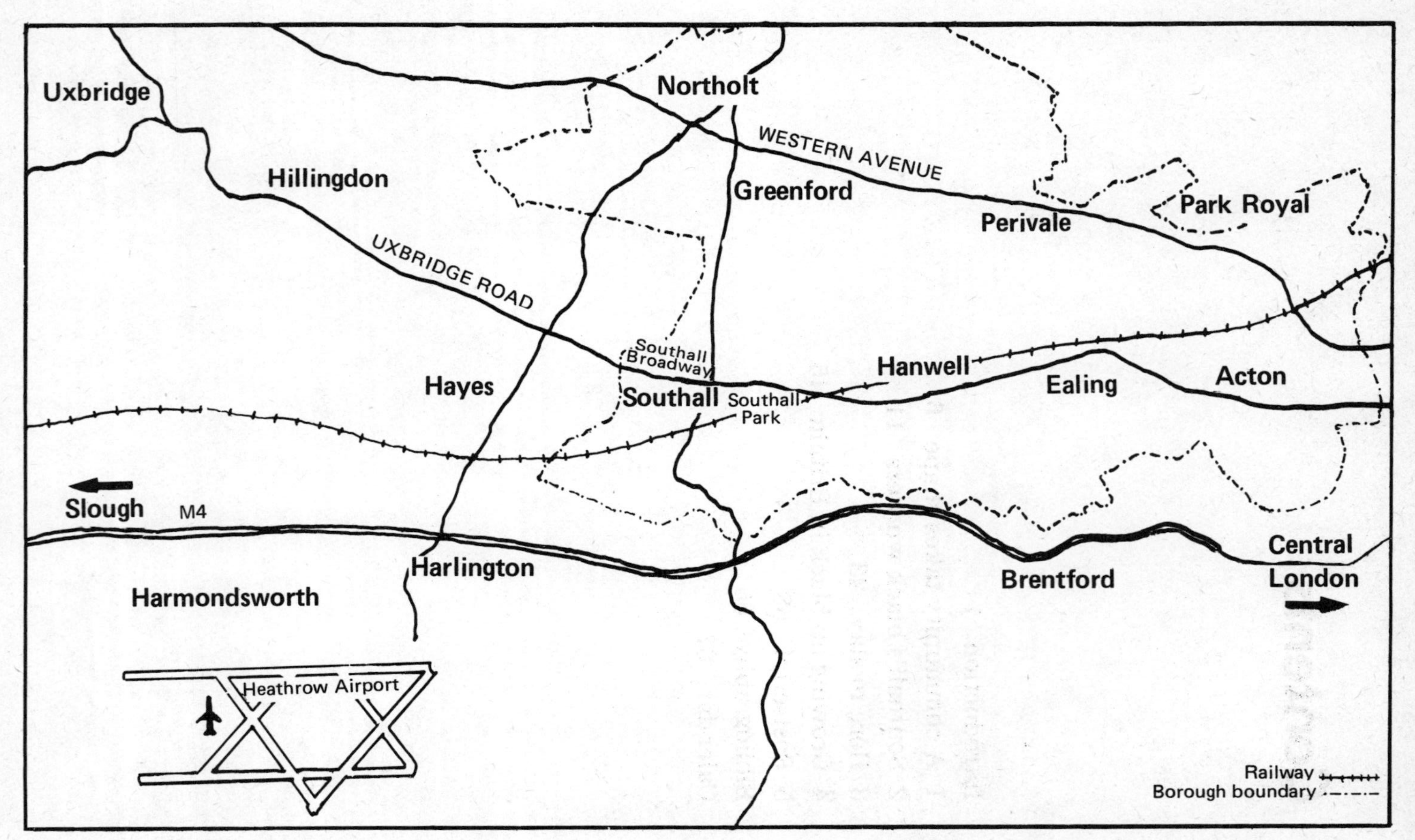
Uxbridge
Northolt
WESTERN AVENUE
Hillingdon
Greenford
Perivale
Park Royal
UXBRIDGE ROAD
Southall Broadway
Hanwell
Hayes
Southall
Southall Park
Ealing
Acton
Slough
M4
Central London
Harlington
Brentford
Harmondsworth
Heathrow Airport
Railway
Borough boundary

Preface

There are many Southalls: black communities built on the rubble of decaying inner cities. This is the story of one of them.

The labour that Britain drew from Asia and the Caribbean helped first to bind its wounds of war and then set it on the road to recovery. Black workers swept and cleaned the cities, ran the transport services, manned – and womanned – the Health Service, worked the foundries, factories and mills, sustaining old industries and helping the new to lift off. They were the aid, the Marshall Plan, on which Britain's immediate post-war prosperity was founded. And yet they themselves were kept from that prosperity, from a stake in that society and, by virtue of the work and housing afforded them, the virtue of their colour, condemned to live midst the detritus of inner cities.

But from those very handicaps – from the 'rocks, moss, stonecrop, iron, merds' of the urban ghetto, against the unwavering racism of governments, employers, unions, police and courts – with little more than the traditions and strengths they had brought with them – black people built themselves their communities.

And it is the knowledge and pride of that achievement that binds the communities of Brick Lane, Brixton, Southall, Moss Side, Lumb Lane, Chapeltown, Handsworth and makes them 'no go' areas for police harassment and fascist tyranny alike.

A. Sivanandan
Director
Institute of Race Relations
July 1981

Acknowledgements
We thank the many people in and around Southall who gave us their opinions and information; the Peter Townsend Trust and the Stichting ter Ondersteuning van geweldloze strijdtegen het racisme for their financial aid; and the Institute of Race Relations for its resources and support.

Introduction

'Members of the local community ... found themselves ... spectators of an occupying force which sealed off the centre of their town, into which the propagators of racial hatred were to be escorted.'

On April 23, 1979, a whole community took to the streets of Southall to protest at the invasion of its town. The aim was to stage a massive sit-down outside Southall Town Hall, where the National Front was to meet that night. Five thousand people had already marched to Ealing Town Hall on the previous day to demonstrate against the projected meeting. On the 23rd local businesses, factories and transport were stopped from 1pm onwards on a half-day strike.

News that the NF was to meet at Southall Town Hall had at first been met with disbelief by local people. The NF had no support in Southall; it had not put up a local candidate there in a general election since 1970. And the idea that the Council could approve such a calculated insult to the local community – to allow into its very midst a fascist group which aimed to deny black people the freedom to live in peace – was unbelievable.

But the Council was determined that the meeting should go ahead. It even flew the Union Jack – adopted by the NF as its symbol – above the Town Hall (and this, on St George's Day). The Home Secretary, Merlyn Rees, and the Prime Minister, James Callaghan, had not been persuaded to intervene. The meeting could not be banned, they said.*

---

*This, in spite of legal precedent for a ban. Brent Council and the Inner London Education Authority, acting on the knowledge that NF meetings were not public, cards having to be shown to stewards (often to the police as well) to gain entry, had both recently refused the NF meeting space.

So the community drew up plans for a peaceful protest. These were discussed with the local police, who apparently accepted them. But on the day, 2,756 police, including Special Patrol Group units, with horses, dogs, vans, riot shields and a helicopter, were sent in to crush the protest. In an unprecedented police operation the whole town centre was declared a 'sterile' area. Everybody within that area was forced out (this led to many arrests) and penned between three double police cordons on the main roads leading to the Town Hall. They were kept there for hours, unable to get closer to the Town Hall or to leave, confused and disorganised, many of the stewards having already been arrested.

The evidence of hundreds of eye-witnesses shows that by late afternoon the police around the three cordons went berserk. Police vans were driven straight at crowds of people, and when they scattered and ran, officers charged after them, hitting out at random. 'What I saw of their behaviour ... reminded me of a gang of drunken hooligans', 'the police were hitting people over the head with truncheons', 'Police horsemen were charging at people ... their long batons (2'6'') were being used to hit people.' A *Daily Telegraph* reporter saw 'several dozen crying, screaming coloured demonstrators ... dragged bodily along Park View Road to the police station ... Nearly every demonstrator we saw had blood flowing from some sort of injury; some were doubled up in pain. Women and men were crying.'

Blair Peach was killed by one immense blow to his head. Clarence Baker (a member of Peoples Unite who, acting as a steward, was photographed in the early afternoon exhorting people to be calm and patient) ended up in intensive care for days with a fractured skull, having been beaten over the head by police.

There were many reported examples of racial abuse during that day, but the following are particularly telling. As a police coach drove off, a policeman inside was seen to hold up a playing card – the ace of spades – to the window. Another officer was seen tracing the words 'NF' on the misted-up window. (And a few days later, an officer was seen writing 'NF' on a poster of Blair Peach.)

The headquarters of Peoples Unite (a community group which brings together young West Indians and Asians in cultural activity and political awareness) was invaded, those inside were forced out through a gauntlet of police wielding truncheons, and then everything in the building was smashed, including PA equipment worth thousands of pounds. (A few weeks later the Council bulldozed the entire building to the ground – years before the scheduled demolition date.)

By these means the protest was stamped out and the way cleared for the NF meeting to go ahead. About 60 members travelled through the eerily empty streets of the town centre (inside the police cordons) to the Town Hall. Some gave Nazi salutes on the doorstep. With an ironic nod to the law, the NF let in four 'members of the public' – though not the correspondent of the 'nigger-loving' *Daily Mirror*. At the meeting, the local candidate pledged the bulldozing of Southall and its replacement by a 'peaceful English hamlet'.

* * *

What brought the whole community of Southall – men and women, the old and the young, Asians, West Indians and white anti-racists – on to the streets on April 23? What had informed that demonstration of solidarity? What were the struggles and experiences of the Southall people, in work, in housing, in the schools and on the streets, that had prepared the way for such a show of common purpose? Why did the state choose Southall to make such a sustained and brutal attack via the police, the courts and the local authority? We set out to answer these questions, and in the process of writing the history of the struggles in one community – Southall – revealed a pattern of racism and resistance from the 1950s to the present day which is echoed in many of Britain's black communities.

In Chapter 1 we look at Southall's first black settlers and their reception by a white society which was only interested in them as units of labour to refurbish Britain's war-torn economy in the 1950s. We show how this early community, which had nowhere else to turn for help and advice, resorted to traditional methods of organisation.

In Chapter 2 we examine the work experience of Southall's community from the 1950s and show how a pattern of self-reliance and support grew up as the white trade union movement failed to take up black workers' grievances.

In Chapter 3 we examine the history of the community in relation to state racism. We show how black settlement – the arrival of the men's wives and children – involved demands for welfare, housing and educational provision not called for by a community of single men. The state was unwilling to provide any facilities and the whites who had to compete with black families for scarce resources blamed them for declining conditions. Instead of coming out firmly against racism, the state (national and local) responded with ad hoc policy decisions intended to allay white fears and which, in effect, laid the basis for a policy of institutional racism. We trace the way that discrimination has been a policy in Southall since the early 1960s, often changing its shape and form but always marking Southall's black residents out for separate and unequal treatment. And we look at Southall's black community's response which has ranged from trying to appease white hostility and complying with racist measures to lobbying and organising against discrimination and building up Southall into a self-contained 'Asian town'. Housing, education, police, immigration and party politics highlight the relationship between state racism and black resistance.

In Chapter 4 we re-examine some of the same history, but from a different viewpoint – that of those who were born or brought up in Southall. The youth, who were at the sharp end of overt state racism (e.g., the bussing policy and police harassment) and of white racialist violence in the schools and on the streets, did not have the same links as their parents, with another country which they could call 'home'. They were to develop new forms of resistance, springing from their experience in England. And it was through the experience of racism that West Indian and Asian youth found common cause and began to organise to protect the community – in the process having to bypass the methods of organising that their elders had pursued. If anything was to vindicate the youths' tactics and put the whole community on their side, it was the brutality of the local authority, the courts and, especially, the police in and after April 1979.

Finally, Chapter 5 assesses the impact of April 23, both nationally and locally. We relate how the day's events and the death of Blair Peach provoked nationwide criticism of the police, and of the SPG in particular, and raised questions about policing which were felt far beyond Southall. Locally, we show how the community, far from being shattered by April 23, came together to organise against both an immediate further assault – this time from the courts – and against further state and racist attacks.

A calendar of events is provided to accompany the text, since to present the analysis in each chapter it was not possible to keep to a strict chronological narrative.

* * *

This pamphlet is about the history of the black communities in Southall, but we are aware that we have concentrated on the Sikhs at the expense of other groups – the East African Asians, the Pakistanis, the West Indians. This is partly a result of the cultural, social and political dominance of the Sikh community, by far the largest group numerically, and partly because of the form of struggle within the different communities.

For example, West Indians in Southall did not organise as West Indians in the employment field, the jobs available to them being scattered throughout the public and private sectors. Many were concentrated in hospitals, canteens and public transport – but, by and large, they worked alongside white workers, albeit in the worst jobs. Unlike the Sikhs they were not normally separated off into particular processes or shifts. There was no clear-cut fight for them against institutionalised racism, and so there was no specifically West Indian organisation on the shop floor for us to report on. West Indian youth, however, did have a specifically racial battle to fight, both in the schools, against racist assessments, ESN schooling and racial attacks (physical and verbal), and on the streets and in the clubs, against direct racialism – so there they were forced to fight as a community.

We are also aware that there are elements which have shaped the Sikh organisations which we have omitted. These are the caste factors in different organisations such as the Temples and within the Indian Workers' Association (IWA), the influence of family/village factors and the impact of allegiances to Indian political parties on the divisions within Southall's politics. We have purposely not researched these complex areas because we do not see it as belonging to our task, which is to expose the history of Southall's struggle as a political lesson for those interested in the history of black communities everywhere.

1 A community takes shape

Southall, now part of the London Borough of Ealing, is a typical example of an industrial conurbation. Based around the old Great Western Railway, about five miles west along the Uxbridge Road from Shepherds Bush, it grew up during the latter decades of the nineteenth century. The older part of the borough, which is centred on the railway station, consists of streets of Victorian terraced houses, some of whose names – Beaconsfield, Salisbury – echo the political personalities of that period.

During the inter-war years, Southall attracted labour from the depressed coal mining areas of South Wales and Durham, as well as from Ireland. After the Second World War, a considerable number of Polish ex-servicemen settled in the area. And it was work that first brought black people to Southall. Post-war Britain had an enormous need for unskilled labour, and in the boom years of the 1950s certain firms around Southall, notably Woolf's Rubber Co., actively sought Asian workers, both to fuel expansion and to fill the gaps left by white workers who, able to move on to better employment, were rejecting the dirty, badly-paid jobs.

Colonialism and the Punjab

Most of the early arrivals were Asian men, young Sikhs from the Jullundhur and Hoshiarpur regions of the Punjab. Though one of the last parts of India to be conquered by Britain, when once in its thrall, the Punjab was developed strictly according to British designs. It became the main recruiting ground for the Indian Army after the mutiny of 1857 and the Punjab's soldiers were to protect British imperial interests all around the globe. After 1857 the landed elite was strengthened and consolidated by the British so as to secure its allegiance, and a class of rich farmers was created by the canal colonisation of the arid zone of West Punjab for British cash crop production, where military pensioners in particular were encouraged to settle.

The new land-holding system introduced by the British had grave consequences socially and economically. Punjabi Sikhs were forced to become migrants, moving both to urban centres and further afield to East Africa, as indentured labourers building railways for the British. And it was the Punjab once again which was to provide the majority of the Indian Army fighting in the Second World War. With the partition of India by Britain in 1947 the Punjab was split between India and Pakistan, and vast numbers of non-Muslims moved into the former. A new category of 'displaced person' intensified economic competition and pressure on land threatened the status of many families. By the early 1950s India's Punjab was one of the smallest states and had one of the most rapidly increasing populations. The 1951 Census showed Jullundhur to have the highest density of population per square mile in the whole Punjab, as well as the highest number of uneconomic landholdings.

It was the marginal landholder, often of the Jat (tiller) caste, who, in mortal fear of becoming landless, gambled his last and came to Britain – selling land, jewellery, cattle or other family possessions, even borrowing, in order to raise the 4,000 rupees needed for the journey.

Southall's first black workers

The Sikh community of Southall started with ex-non commissioned army officers and educated unemployed Punjabi pioneers. In the 1951 Census, out of a total population of 55,896, only 330 were recorded as being from the Commonwealth. In the early 1950s the majority of Southall's Asian workers were of peasant origin, with a steady trickle of the Punjab's intelligentsia (clerks, teachers and petty officials). Initially, they commuted from other areas of London (especially Aldgate in east London) to work in the Southall area at Woolf's Rubber Co., two bakeries and, later, at Nestles and Batchelors canning factory.

Some West Indians, commuting from North Kensington and Willesden, also found work in the Southall area. In the main, they were offered employment (in particular, in transport and the hospitals) which kept them apart from the Asian workers. They were a far smaller community than the Punjabis. In 1958, out of a total population of 55,000 in Southall, 1,250 were Asian and 150 Jamaican. There was also a small, but growing, community of Pakistanis, mainly from the Mirpur and Sylhet districts of undivided Pakistan and, to a lesser extent, Lahore.

'No coloured please'

In the early days the Asian community in Southall was made up of young men who had come to Britain with the idea of earning enough money to improve their position at home – for example, by buying their land if they were merely tenants, or by investing in a tractor to increase the yield. In fact, all their meagre earnings were taken up with feeding, clothing and housing themselves and sending some money home regularly to support their families. A 60-hour working week was considered quite normal, and some put in 75 hours, working seven days a week. Employers welcomed this, but it made commuting from the East End or elsewhere impossibly time-consuming, as well as costly. The obvious thing was to move to where the work was.

> *TO LET: Decent single bed-sitting room with facilities to cook in basement kitchen. Suit a working gentleman or woman. Only respectable people need apply. No coloured please.*
>
> *Advert in Southall shop (1958)*

Accommodation was very hard to find. There was no question of either the companies who were profiting from the men's labour or the local authority providing housing for them. Few whites were willing to let to black people, and there were very few Asians or West Indians with enough capital to buy houses. Those that did filled them rapidly with co-workers desperate for a bed. So the accommodation that was available became overcrowded, sometimes grossly so. 'You cannot imagine how barbarously we lived in those days', recalls an Indian worker. 'The front room had three beds, two of them double. The back room had a similar number. The two other bedrooms on the first floor had five beds; the large front room four beds. The number of people there fluctuated between twenty and twenty-five. Some of the beds were used during the day by the night shift workers, and at night by the day workers.'

The shortage of accommodation and the common experience of discrimination brought the communities together from the first. Irish and Indian workers struck up friendships in lodging houses, finding a bond in their colonial history and a common distrust of the English. West Indians and Asians also became close. 'There were few of us and we would stick together, rent from each other, as whites wouldn't let to us.'

Within the Sikh community, mutual reliance and help were both essential and natural – essential because 45 per cent of the men were unable to speak any English, and natural because the men all came from a fairly small area, often from the same village, and knew each other; many were blood relations. Thus an informal network of mutual aid was established.

The 20 per cent who spoke fluent English became the interpreters and leaders. Indians in Southall were concentrated in an area with only half-an-hour's walking distance between its furthest points, so in an emergency, or even in the normal course of life, whenever help was required it could be readily obtained from friends or relatives in the neighbourhood. The educated or experienced people helped in interpreting and filling in forms, the influential in arranging employment and accommodation for newcomers. An overwhelming proportion of the men were employed in a few factories, so work experiences were similar and lunch breaks and travelling time were spent in each other's company. Southall Park and the grounds of the Manor House became meeting points on a Sunday, where the men would exchange news and information about contacts with white workers, factory managements and working conditions. In the factories, too, they relied very much on each other's cooperation.

Because of the small area from which most of the Sikhs came, they could discuss problems arising at home with the same ease and familiarity. An Asian anthropologist reconstructed a conversation at that time: 'Natha gets a letter from home. They have received the money he sent to them and now they are planning to buy some land which is being sold by one of the neighbours. But that would require some more money. He comes and tells his *beli* (childhood friend), Makhan, and asks his advice. Makhan knows which land Natha is talking about. The land is good but is irrigated by a well, which means that a bullock would be needed to work the well. Can Natha afford another bullock?'

Community solidarity

Out of these informal groupings of friends and relatives the first community organisations emerged. The Indian Workers' Association was formed in Southall on 3 March, 1957, by some of the younger, more radical elements in the Punjabi community. The older men had already formed the Indo-Pakistan Cultural Society, to do educational work in the community. Each Sunday, from 12am to 5pm, the IWA and IPCS showed Indian films in hired halls – the proceeds of which went towards English classes and Indian newspapers which were put in the IWA centre. In 1959 Southall had its own *Gurdwara* (Sikh Temple). Until then Sikhs had travelled into London to attend the Temple there. Both the IWA and the *Gurdwara* played a vital role in these early days. As no British agency – national or local, statutory or voluntary – was doing anything to help in the provision of housing, or even advice, on arrival a man would go to the IWA (which in 1962 rented its own premises in Featherstone Road) or to the *Gurdwara*. There, he found help with temporary accommodation, advice on possible employers and assistance in house purchase, filling in forms and so on. From its inception the IWA also worked at forging links with other black workers and bridging religious and national divisions in the community. Thus it gave associate membership to Pakistani workers.

West Indian workers, too were not slow to organise in the face of discrimination in housing. For them the main problems were exorbitant rents and immediate eviction if they complained at the appalling conditions they had to live in. They called a meeting to expose the worst landlords (and to root out and censure those of their own community who were exploiting their countrymen's misery), and to make plans to work together as a community. From this first meeting the West Indian Association (later known as the Afro-Caribbean Association) was formed.

2 Southall's black workers

In the 1950s work was plentiful and local employers encouraged Asian workers to send for their friends and relatives. New arrivals could find jobs in Southall, at Woolf's or Krafts, or in the neighbouring areas of Hayes, Greenford, Perivale, Feltham, West Drayton, Uxbridge, Slough, Hounslow and Brentford. Heathrow Airport became a large employer of Asians, despite poor conditions, partly because of the concessionary tickets given on long-distance routes. The hospitals around Southall (St Bernards and Hillingdon) also provided many jobs.

In the main, the work that was available was all of a type – defined not by craft or skill but as the work white people would no longer do. It entailed long, irregular hours, shift work, dirty, hot or damp conditions, monotonous tasks, lower than average wages, strict discipline, lack of promotion and little or no job security. The industrial belt around Southall did, however, provide a very different work experience from that of the East End rag-trade sweatshops. No tiny back-room workshops for the Southall settlers (at least, not for the men), but large, expanding factories, often in the newer industries (plastics, rubber, man-made textiles, food processing).

With Asian labour on the shifts that local white workers would not do, management found the means to get the most out of its machinery, running it 24 hours a day. Asian workers also often found themselves in types of job or parts of a process which cut them off and marked them out from white workers. It was because of this segregation – this concentration on shifts and in certain work – that they found the need to organise themselves not just as workers, but as black workers and to deal with issues that their union (if there was one) ignored.

The response of the local trade unions to the new force of workers was, initially, neither threatening nor welcoming. There were no strikes against the employment of black workers (which did occur in other areas), but neither were there drives for large-scale union recruitment nor any attempts to take up disparities between white and black workers in pay, hours and conditions. When Asian workers started to organise themselves, however, and actively sought union help in fighting disparities, union indifference turned into positive lack of support, even betrayal.

The Asian response

The strikes of Asian workers in and around Southall have been many and militant and spanned many types of industry: Woolf's, Rockware Glass, Lyons Maid, Dura Tube Wire, Chibnall Bakery, Injection Moulding, Wynuna Corset, Combined Optical Industries, Perivale Gutterman, Artid Plastics, Crown Cork, Booth's Gin, Mother's Pride, Heathrow Airport, Chix, Investacast and Meaden Plastics.

Insulated though they were, Asian workers were often in the vanguard of industrial disputes, raising issues, such as union recognition, which would also benefit white co-workers – but the latter showed no interest, let alone solidarity. The Asian workers did not lack a knowledge of procedure or need lessons from the British trade union movement. Amongst the early Asian settlers were a few who had been actively engaged in Indian political life, and had already participated in industrial struggles in the capitalised sector of the Punjab. When support was not forthcoming from their white fellow workers, they turned to traditional sources of support in their own community. This was born out of totally different conditions in India, where the rural areas surrounding the small urban centres had given free food and support to workers on strike. In Southall the same pattern emerged – shopkeepers gave food on credit or gave it free, landlords waived the rent for a few weeks and the *Gurdwara* made collections on behalf of the strikers. Out of necessity, a tradition of self-reliance as a community developed. Though few of the industrial struggles resulted in 'victory', they were to add a further dimension to the sense of strength and confidence of the black community.

We present here four disputes to illustrate the responses of the Asian workers to their position at the bottom of the pile and the inability of the unions to grapple with racism and/or fight for their black members. We look at Asian workers (male and female) in struggle at different points in time, and in different types of employment – production and the service sector. Though the unions in time have had to accommodate to a permanent black presence in the workforce, racism remains institutionalised at the workplace and Asian workers still have recourse to their own forms of struggle.

The first strike we have examined, at Woolf's in Southall, was perhaps the most significant. It was one of the very first strikes of black workers in Britain (and the longest), and the methods of Asian organisation and struggle were to provide a model and inspiration for later disputes throughout the country.

The second strike, at Perivale Gutterman nearly ten years later, was another dispute which had a national impact. But this time it was part of a wave of strikes of Asian workers in light manufacturing industries up and down the country, including Mansfield Hosiery and Imperial Typewriters. In such firms, discrimination against the Asian section of the workforce had become built into the work situation. The Perivale dispute demonstrated the racialism entrenched in the white workforce and the institutionalised racism in the trade union structure.

We then examine Heathrow Airport, which is currently the largest employer of Southall labour and has witnessed numerous struggles by its Asian women workers in the cleaning and catering section to end discriminatory practices by the employer (or contractor), the union and fellow white workers.

Finally, we look in detail at the Wynuna Corset Company, chosen by a group of Southall women as a target for unionisation. This was no random dispute but part of a calculated campaign to resist the gross exploitation of Southall's women workers in local garment manufacturing and laundries.

Woolf's

In the late 1950s and 1960s Woolf's was the most important place of employment for Southall's Asian workers. In 1960 it employed 40 per cent of the Sikhs of Southall, and by 1965 90 per cent of its unskilled workers were Sikh. Being one of the first factories to hire Asian workers on a large scale (in fact, it attracted them to the area), it dominated the Asian community at that time. Woolf's a family firm, thrived on cheap labour – poor whites from Wales and the North-East in the 1930s, the Poles after the war, and then the Sikhs. The factory made rubber accessories for the motor industry and for prams. The use of carbon black and sulphur made the work extremely unpleasant. Wages were low, conditions bad and work hard. A 60-hour week was considered normal, and large amounts of overtime had to be worked to bring home a living wage – some would work a 7-day week, of 75 hours. Bribery of foremen, to get a job or to keep it and to get overtime, was rife. The management was militantly anti-union, but in 1958 and 1960 attempts were made through the Amalgamated Engineering Union and the Transport & General Workers' Union (TGWU) to unionise. These failed and the organisers were sacked. Efforts were also hampered by the attitude of white workers, who were not keen on joining a 'black' union branch.

In 1963 five members of the IWA executive who were working on the shop floor used their position to recruit intensively for the TGWU. Since this could not be done in the factory, they organised hundreds by going from door to door in the community and winning over each worker by explanation and discussion. With a number of out-of-hours meetings in the community, the practice of bribery was stopped and in 1964 the men won recognition for the union.

Later in the same year the men came out on strike after one of them was dismissed for insulting a white charge-hand. Their action, unsupported by the TGWU, succeeded in re-instating the man. In 1965 a procedure agreement was drawn up, immediately to be broken by management, who sacked ten active union members. The men started a go-slow, threatened other action and waited for the union to act. But it did nothing and in November the men's patience snapped after another unjustified sacking. So they came out. The union pledged its support but paid no strike pay and seemed confused as to whether or not the strike was official – TGWU lorries crossed the picket line. The Asian shop stewards had to struggle with the union at the same time as taking on management.

And there was yet another problem. The management tried to recruit more Pakistanis to the workforce from Luton, High Wycombe and even Bradford – a personnel officer admitted that they tried to divide the workforce along 'ethnic' lines. Tension was running high at the factory gates and one evening a fight developed and the police were called. The IWA and Pakistani Welfare Association leadership worked together to calm the situation. An appeal was written to Pakistanis, asking them to support the strike.*

During the strike, which lasted seven weeks, the IWA allowed strikers to use its office facilities and appealed to landlords to forego rent and to grocers to extend credit. £1,500 was collected in the community for the strike fund. But the IWA was involved in buying the Dominion Cinema for its cultural activities, so its intensive support and mobilisation of fuller community resources was not forthcoming.

In January 1966 the strike ended. Active unionists were not taken back and the other strikers were downgraded. The men protested and many refused to return under such conditions, but the union refused to support their demand for reinstatement without victimisation. TGWU organisation came to an end at the factory – which itself never recovered from the loss of orders during the strike and collapsed the following year.

The lesson learned from this and subsequent strikes was militancy, not anti-unionism. During the strike at Chibnall Bakery in Hayes, Indian workers handed back their strike pay to the union, provoking the wistful comment from a Baker's Union official, 'I wish we had that kind of support from our English workers.'

The long struggle waged at Woolf's is still talked about in Southall. Nearly every Asian family has a connection with the factory – one or more of the family worked there, or a friend. The final closure of the firm is seen as a well-deserved defeat of a super-exploitative management.

Perivale Gutterman

Gutterman's, also a family firm, at Perivale, expanded into the most modern textile plant in Europe through the exploitation of

---

*Community leaders had to intervene again during 1973 when management at Perivale Gutterman used the Indo-Pakistan war to try to inflame communal divisions in the workforce.

Asian labour. Initially the firm eagerly recruited Asians, saying it preferred one Indian or Pakistani worker to ten Italians. Using the family image, it even got Asian workers to work free on Sundays to get the firm back on its feet after a fire – and this despite low wages, dirty working conditions and a long working week. Asian workers made up the majority of manual workers in the factory and Gutterman's owed its success directly to them.

In 1973, when the management wanted to introduce new machinery and demanded double productivity, there was a go-slow which was given official union backing. Management responded by victimisation and the workers replied with a one-day strike. The management then suspended workers for three days and introduced a non-negotiable contract of employment. Then the all-out strike began on 30 November, 1973, following which 70 men were dismissed. The TGWU district branch supported the strike call, but no strike pay was forthcoming until 19 February, 1974. This lack of support at the top also meant no solidarity from other sections of the workforce such as the dockers, who could have hit the firm hard by refusing to handle its exports. And, already faced with the three-day week local trade unionists gave scant assistance. The workers turned once again to their communities for help. Both the Indian and Pakistani workers' associations organised collections and the *Gurdwara* asked local shops to supply men on strike with free sugar, flour, oil and essential groceries. Without all this, the strike would certainly have collapsed within weeks. The Department of Employment sent new workers down, lorries crossed picket lines and by March management had got back to 70 per cent of its former production.

Before this dispute the TGWU, like most other unions, had a policy of non-cooperation with the Industrial Relations Act's machinery. But now it adopted the reverse policy and left the cases of the 70 dismissed workers to be decided by the National Industrial Relations Court. Management used this to prevaricate and the hearing of the case was postponed for two months. Finally, on 5 April, the Industrial Tribunal ruled against the 70 men. The strike was beaten. Having abandoned the strikers, the TGWU abandoned the factory. Union organisation only started up again in November 1975, when new Asian stewards launched a recruitment campaign.

Women in the workforce

The women came to join their husbands in Britain from the early 1960s onwards, when it became clear that for the men a short stay was not a viable proposition. Their previous experience of work was in terms of the household and its relationship to the land. Women worked on the land, fetched the water and tended the animals as well as organising the domestic world of the home. There was no division – as there is in the West – because the household and the land were one. The question of waged work outside the home did not arise.

Life in Southall was different. The men's wages were not enough to support the family, and economic necessity impelled the women to look for paid work outside the home. At first, this meant working behind the scenes in restaurants and shops owned or run by a relative; later they moved into small firms, also Asian owned, and small sweatshops. But as the community became established, they began to move further afield, to the food processing industries around Southall (Lyons Maid, Walls, Nestles, Associated Biscuits) and to large laundries and garment factories (Brentford Nylons, Wynuna) and to the service sectors of Heathrow Airport and the local hospitals.

Women of all ages could be found at the same workplace, introduced there by a relative or a friend. Since they often spoke little English and were unfamiliar with the work, the women were given the least skilled and worst paid jobs wherever they were. And more often than not they found themselves in all-female, and all-Asian shifts. This in fact made the work bearable for them, re-creating some of the traditional female sources of support that living in a western capitalised society tended to erode. But it was also ideal for management. Isolated from the rest of the workforce or set on a level below Asian men or white women, unused to an industrial setting, the Asian women were not in a position to question wages or conditions, or try to organise. Where they did belong to unions, they were often as unclear about which it was as they were about their conditions of employment and the statutory rates of pay – and union officials never took the trouble to involve them or speak to their specific problems. The majority, however, worked in sectors which were not unionised, and feared that joining a union, which they tended to associate solely with strikes, would result in instant dismissal.

(This had indeed happened in 1967 during an ill-organised strike, promoted by the TGWU, for increased pay for women cleaners at Heathrow.) But through the unremitting work of a handful of women – Asian and white – who won the trust of the Asian women workers, initially around such basic demands as language training (incorporating within this information about union practice and procedure), the role of Asian women in industrial disputes has changed dramatically in the last decade.

Hard though their lives were – with domestic chores to look to when they got home, with worries about child-minding when there were no relatives at hand to help (Southall had next to no nursery provision) and unfamiliar with industrial organisation – the female Asian workforce gradually disproved the myth of their docility. From 1967 right up the Chix strike of 1980, Asian women have been part of the militant black workers' tradition of Southall.

Heathrow

Heathrow Airport is the largest service complex in Britain, employing over 57,000 people. Since the 1960s it has been the largest employer of Southall's Asian women, who work in the cleaning and catering divisions.* Both involve unpleasant, hard and dirty jobs – and a hierarchy of these, with Asian women at the bottom. For example, in the cleaning department, the relatively popular job of lavatory attendant (favoured because of the tips which supplement the low wages) was until recently monopolised by whites.

Cleaners at Heathrow are employed by contractors, who submit tenders to the British Airports Authority. The BAA, concerned simply with maximising profit, accepts the lowest tender, without checking to see if the contractor has a fair wage clause. Acme Industrial Cleaners has held a contract for many years. In 1980, cleaners earned only £1.18 per hour on round-the-clock shifts, which means either getting up at 4 a.m. to catch the company bus, or leaving home or returning to it late at night. Acme keeps its employees weak and unable to fight effectively for

---

*Asian men from Southall work mainly in portering jobs, with only a few in catering. Entry into the skilled jobs in engineering and maintenance has been difficult, largely because of discrimination in recruitment and also through union reluctance. And as cuts squeeze jobs, black workers are the first out, even from the unskilled jobs.

changes by sacking them periodically and then re-employing them in another terminal. Making use of the women's inability to understand English, it has them sign 'admissions of misconduct' which are held against them if they try to take their case to an Industrial Tribunal.

The TGWU has turned a blind eye to practices such as this, and to the violation of agreements by managements. A strike for more pay in 1967 led to the sacking of 40 women, but the TGWU has done nothing to convince the women that it is on their side. The cleaners are now turning to community organisations like Southall Rights in an effort to ascertain their rights in relation to Acme, and other similar firms like Reliance, and to fight against arbitrary dismissal and sharp practices by the management.

The hierarchy in the catering section has at least meant that Asian women work together in one place, rather than spread throughout the huge complex, and so organisation has been easier to achieve. The main grievance in catering has been the disparity between white and black catering workers. White women, called 'assistant cooks', work in the kitchen, packing prepared food onto trays for inflight meals. The Asian women, called 'catering attendants', work outside the kitchen, packing the cutlery, cups, plates and napkins onto the same trays, and are paid some £10 a week less. While the white women can go at their own pace, the Asians work on a conveyor belt line and can take no breaks – except half an hour for lunch and 10 minutes for tea – from their task of packing 4,000 or more trays a day. The Asian women complain that the supervisors – all white – bully them, make racialist remarks and treat them like children. The regrading of the jobs (for they were not always so differentiated) appears to have taken place when Asian women started working in catering in the mid 1960s – and it has been fought over since 1969.

The TGWU's attitude has been the same towards the catering workers as to the cleaners. It did nothing to stop the practice whereby people who had worked at Heathrow for years were classed as 'temporary' (by the simple device of dismissing and re-employing them periodically), and were thus ineligible for promotion, etc. It did not protest against the regrading of the jobs by management and turned a blind eye to the low wages and discriminatory treatment. Whenever the Asian women's demands became too loud to be ignored, the senior TGWU official would rush to the scene to guarantee that disparities would be sorted out 'within six months'. This went on until 1975, when 450 Asian workers walked out on their own initiative. The union declared the strike unofficial. Without its support, the women could not survive a long strike and went back after a week.

But they had won more concessions during that one week than the union had achieved for them in the previous six years. The practice of temporary employment was stopped and a free meal was promised. But the issue of parity was not resolved.

In the same year, the catering shop stewards submitted a detailed report to the Race Relations Board setting out the discriminatory practices in recruitment and promotion (unqualified white women inevitably being promoted over the heads of senior, experienced and qualified Asians), as well as the regrading system and the disparities in pay and conditions between white and black workers. Although the report showed clearly that racial discrimination was the norm, nothing ever came out of it.

The catering workers' militancy has not decreased since 1975. In spite of the lack of union support and in spite of management making and breaking promises, they are still fighting.

Wynuna

Towards the end of 1972 the IWA Southall called a meeting in which a local woman worker talked about the problems facing Indian and Pakistani women. She spoke of the appalling working conditions and low wages of many Asian women working in local laundries, sewing factories and the airport and as cleaners and homeworkers. Out of this came a group of about ten women determined to do something. After many meetings and discussions they decided to make a start by helping to unionise one clothing factory.

In Southall, clothing factories were almost exclusively staffed by Asian women who, from a management point of view, were a 'good buy'. They worked hard, often through lunch breaks, and accepted wages well below the average. The low pay and level of exploitation, a throw-back to Dickensian times, was resented by the local trade unionists who felt that the women were eroding the gains they had made and were exacerbating racial hostility among white semi-skilled workers who perceived the women as undercutting them.

The clothing factory chosen for unionisation had to be large and financially sound, for the group wanted a victory big enough to be noticed, but not a closure. Wynuna Corset Company sewing factory at Gladstone Road, Southall, which a company search revealed to be financially sound, was selected. For its workforce of over 100 Asian women conditions were bad and rates of pay unknown; piece-work was the norm and there were fines for 'bad workmanship'.

The organisation of the women, a covert and community-based affair (like Woolf's before), was long and difficult. The women had to be contacted individually at home. At first they were suspicious, afraid of losing their jobs and hostile to outside interference. A handful of the original group, mainly Asians, persisted. They received some outside support, but it was through their own determination that finally three of the women workers agreed to join a union if others did. At that point the TGWU let them down, showing no interest in these potential new members. But the Tailor & Garment Workers' Union West London organiser provided appropriate agreements, wage rates, etc., and agreed to sign the Wynuna workers up as members.

By February 1973 rumours were already spreading around the factory that people were joining the union. As a few joined, others were slowly encouraged to follow. The first union meeting, consisting of 20 members, was secret. By June there were 45 recruits and the union organiser felt strong enough to confront the management for recognition. Meanwhile, plans were made to picket Dorothy Perkins shops if recognition was not granted and an article exposing the situation was placed in a sympathetic newspaper. This jolted the management and after a few weeks, it agreed to recognise the union. The women elected their stewards and conditions and wages began to improve.

* * *

Many other struggles involving Asian women have gone unrecorded. Not all involved strikes. They have fought for language training schemes and for nursery provision, facilities which not only better their working conditions but also improve their bargaining position – for time and some knowledge of English are essentials for organisation.

Through their struggles the Asian women of Southall have

developed a degree of organisation that was witnessed in the half day strike of April 23, 1979. Women in some local factories, anxious to take part in protecting their community against the fascists, were determined to be there that afternoon. Knowing that management would not only refuse them time off, but would also dock their pay, they adopted a concerted plan. Stating that they were afraid of the fascists and of getting caught up with them on their way home, they insisted on being bussed back to Southall. So management got them back in time to take to the streets with the rest of the community.

3 Here to stay

In Chapter 1 we described the beginnings of a community in the late 1950s – a community which was then almost entirely composed of men, with no intention of settling in Britain for good. In Chapter 2 we looked at Southall's Asian community as workers – for work was what they came for, and was what brought them to Southall. But in describing the struggles in the employment field and the development of community solidarity there, we have had to jump ahead of our story. In taking it up again, we now start to chart the processes whereby the migrant workers became settlers, and the reactions to this by government at local and national level. We then relate how the growing community responded to indifference, neglect and hostility – from white institutions, and from white society at large.

As the men found that discrimination not only kept them in the worst paid jobs but also extorted the highest rents from them, the idea of making a large sum of money and taking it home gave way to the need to stay for longer and to save in order to bring their families over (as quickly as possible in view of the increasingly stringent immigration controls that successive governments passed from 1962 onwards).

As workers, the men had been welcomed as units of cheap labour in an expanding economy. Their needs – accommodation, health, language training – had been ignored both by central and local government (in contrast to the Resettlement Schemes set up by post-war governments to aid Polish and Central European settlers). The men were left to fend for themselves. But the arrival of the men's wives and children, from the beginning of the 1960s onwards, brought about a change in official attitudes. Family settlement meant a demand on housing, educational, social and welfare services – all in an already neglected area. Those that felt the competition for services were the white working-class families in the same areas and they, responding to the politicians' and mass media's racist demands for immigration controls, soon scapegoated the black families as the *cause* of their problems. And the 'policies' which emerged at local level in the early 1960s were not those of providing services for black families and helping them to settle but ad hoc responses directed towards allaying 'white fears'.

For a contradiction had been thrown up for the state between the social and the economic needs of Britain – the super-profit from exploiting black labour would be reduced if facilities had to be made for the reproduction of black families, and yet political dissatisfaction of white working-class people (who were in effect bearing the infrastructural cost of immigration) had to be kept within bounds. It was this realisation, coupled with the fact that the economic boom was over, so that the need for black labour was abating, which led to control of entry via immigration acts. This legislation, deliberately setting out to exclude black people from Britain – implying therefore that they were a problem to be kept at bay – was to begin the systematic treatment of black families as second class, by national and local government, and by other bodies, such as the police.

The struggle for housing

Since the end of the war housing had been scarce in Southall; the expansion of industry meant more people and the housing stock was old and inadequate. Most of central Southall was built in the late nineteenth and early twentieth centuries, and lacked proper sanitation and basic amenities. As better and more expensive houses went up in the 'green areas' around Southall, some white owners could afford to sell up and move out of the decaying centre, and it was here that the new settlers came. Here, too, was where they bought houses in anticipation of having their wives and children with them – there was no chance of council housing.

A house was seen as a good investment, many of the Asians having a traditional bias for land, which back home represented security. But it was an expensive solution for the poorly paid workers, who had to support families back home while they saved up the fares to bring them here. And it was made more expensive by the discrimination they encountered. Often mortgages had to be raised from unscrupulous dealers, as neither the local borough council nor established estate agents or mortgage brokers were prepared to help. In many cases private mortgages had to be arranged, with high interest rates and high repayments. To raise the money, many turned to their kin for help. Money was pooled, or borrowed from friends or relatives, people from the same village back home, or people in the same workplace, to put down the deposit on a house or occasionally even buy one outright. This would then provide rented accommodation for others until they too could get the money together to buy a house.

The white backlash

These arrangements often led to three or four families having to live in one small house. And it was the twin issues of overcrowding and house-buying by Asians that were to be explosive in Southall during the early 1960s. Racialists were quick to seize the political capital in overcrowding, making the immigrants, not the conditions they had to live in, the 'health hazard', and they spread fears of 'swamping' by hordes of Asian house-buyers. In 1959 a delegation of 20 residents asked the Council to 'stop coloured people from buying property in the area'. With their platform of 'Send them back', the British National Party (BNP) campaigned on this issue in the 1963 local elections where, with 27 per cent of the vote, they pushed the Tories into third place in the Hambrough Ward.

The Labour Council jumped right on to the racial bandwagon. (One prominent Labour councillor had for years made no secret of his views, blaming the immigrants for 'ruining my native Southall' and supporting the Tories in their stand against immigration.) It set up a sub-committee to deal with the 'problems of multi-occupation by immigrants', which resulted, not in any recommendation to build more houses or otherwise alleviate the situation, but in prosecutions for overcrowding. And when hundreds of angry white residents, calling for 'peace and quiet, not Indians', mobbed the Council in 1963, demanding that it 'stop the silent invasion' by compulsory purchase of vacant houses to prevent immigrants buying them, the Council obliged. It bought a house already viewed by eight Indian families, and sold it to a white buyer. At the same time it called on George Pargiter,

Southall's Labour MP, to urge the Home Secretary to legislate against the further entry of immigrants into 'towns such as Southall, already overcrowded and saturated with immigrants'.

Spurred by this success, white residents formed the Southall Residents' Association (SRA) in October 1963. Led by ex-BNP candidate Arthur Cooney and local Conservative Mrs Penn (who resigned soon after on discovering it to be a racialist organisation!), its members pressured the Council to take more action about the 'problems arising from the undesirable elements in our midst' and specifically about overcrowding. The Council pointed out that it had already served 369 notices, forcing landlords to get rid of tenants on pain of prosecution – and between then (October) and the end of that year it was to serve another 70.

The IWA's view, that the main problem was the lack of any building programme, and that improvement grants would be a more constructive solution than prosecutions for overcrowding, received scant attention in the local press and short shrift from the Council. In October 1963 representatives of the IWA, the Indian High Commission and the Jamaican Migrants Adviser met with the Council and reiterated that the main problem was shortage of housing – but the Council did not want to know. In December it pressed ahead with a stricter definition of overcrowding (from 8-10 to 5-7 people per dwelling), without giving notice to community leaders of its intentions, and refused the IWA's request for more time to enable landlords and tenants to make adjustments.

In February 1964 the Mayor accepted an invitation to the IWA's Indian Independence Day celebrations, only to abuse this act of goodwill by issuing a public warning to Southall's immigrant population about overcrowding. 'You will abide by the standards we lay down', he said.

Thus the official attitude in the early days to the housing needs of the black community was punitive, forcing evictions through prosecutions for overcrowding. No positive steps were taken to rehouse evicted families; the Council considered its duty done once the offending households were cut down to size, and neither knew nor cared where the homeless went.

Creation of a ghetto

The first indication of an even harder-line policy towards

Southall's black population came in 1965. By then many Asian and West Indian families were eligible for council housing, and although few applied, most preferring to buy their own home if possible, those few were enough to provoke alarm on the Council (now Ealing Borough Council under the local government reorganisation). The Tories proposed a motion calling for a 15-year residence qualification for blacks to go on the housing list – as against five years for whites. Five Labour councillors crossed the floor to support the motion. However, it was defeated, and the five were expelled from the Labour Party (two of them then joined the SRA). For Labour in central government was attempting a delicate balancing act (1965 was the year of the first Race Relations Act) and such open racism was not politic as regards Britain's settled black population. But the motion reflected a desire on the part of both parties on the Council to do as little as possible about Southall's increasingly acute housing problem – an attitude which has persisted up to the present.

Under the force of this neglect, Southall's housing problem became the worst in the Borough. Numerous reports from the late 1960s onwards chronicled the decay of the town's ageing housing stock, and the appalling, insanitary and overcrowded conditions families were forced to live in. Since the late 1960s almost every national survey has reported that the two central Southall wards, Glebe and Northcote, have one of the highest incidence of overcrowded houses in the country.

The problem began to assume crisis proportions in the early 1970s when the price of a modest family house soared from £3,000-£5,000 to as much as £15,000 over a period of about three years. This meant that the possibility of buying a house receded for most families, and the equally pressing shortage of private rented accommodation forced many more to put their names down on the Council's waiting list. A Labour administration made a start on the problem by building a 700-unit estate on Southall's northern borders with Greenford in 1972, and even a small flat in one of its bleak and windswept tower blocks was infinitely preferable to living five or six to a damp, cold room. But this start was never followed up. Since then new building in Southall has dried up almost totally.

In 1977 the Housing (Homeless Persons) Act imposed a duty on local councils to re-house homeless people in the Borough. This increased the housing burden on the Council but, contrary to expectations, did not spark off the much-needed spending on Southall's housing. The reverse happened. The Council reduced the rates in 1977/8, at a time when other London boroughs were imposing massive rises to offset the effect of central government cuts on their housing programmes. The Labour administration's housing spokesman explained the decision thus: 'The citizenry as a whole would not have welcomed rates rises which were to go into housing' – which, in the context of a borough whose most pressing housing problems are in Southall, can only be interpreted as 'the white voters wouldn't like us spending money on blacks'.

Labour's attitude when in power meant that the Tories had very little difficulty with them in opposition. Taking over in 1978, they continued to reduce the rates right up to 1981, and continued the policy, bequeathed them by Labour, of underspending the housing budget. In 1978/9 the underspending on central government's housing grant allocation was a massive 30 per cent, in 1979/80 15 per cent. Even the demands made on central government for funds were derisory, compared with inner-city Boroughs with similar housing problems. One of the most frequently heard excuses for the appalling neglect of Southall is that there just isn't the space for new housing. Yet one of the largest of the Borough's nine golf courses spreads from the High Street right to the Greenford borders, and the Council has been selling off land in Southall for years to commercial concerns, for warehousing.

This refusal to build new houses, coupled with the Council's policy of selling land and council housing to private buyers and its extra re-housing responsibilities imposed by the 1977 Act, mean that no one is now being re-housed from the waiting list, which in 1980 had some 1,500 Southall families on it. Nor is the Council pursuing so mercilessly its overcrowding prosecutions – for now it has a duty to re-house those it makes homeless. This means that overcrowding is on the increase, with many families living four or six to a room. And if the Council can find a way of evading its statutory responsibility, it will do so. An Indian man, resident here for over 20 years, was evicted from his room, together with his two children, and refused re-housing under the Homeless Persons Act, on the grounds that he was intentionally homeless since he had a part-share of a house in India.

So, for many families in Southall the wheel has turned full

circle. In the 1950s husbands had to separate from their wives and children to come to Britain to earn a living. Now, in many cases, wives and children stay with relatives and there is simply no room for the husband, who has to sleep somewhere else. Families who have been at the top of the Council waiting list for years are no nearer being offered housing than when they first put their names down. The Tories' attitude is summed up in the words of their housing spokesman, Councillor Woods, who said in November 1980: 'If Southall families don't want to live in poor conditions, they will have to get out of the borough.'

Community action

Housing is not the only need to have been systematically ignored through the years. Repeated pleas for better car parking facilities have been disregarded, and the resultant on-street parking and daily traffic snarl-ups in the congested streets have caused many injuries and several deaths to local children. To make matters worse, a lorry park is now being planned for a central site, in the middle of busy shopping and residential streets. The local hospital was closed in 1979, and although there is the giant new Ealing Hospital on the outskirts of Southall, it has no maternity facilities. Southall women have to travel to Perivale for these.

There has been a lot of anger in Southall about the attitude of the Council, but the piecemeal nature of the problem has made mass mobilisation difficult. And the political traditions that the first settlers brought with them were those of lobbying, petitioning and working through the elders. They adopted the same measures here to work for change and to make their presence felt within the decision-making bodies. In 1967 the first Asian councillor was elected, and since then Southall has returned several – Labour and independent. But their small numbers on the Council have made it impossible for them to do anything more than protest at the policy of deliberate neglect.

Direct action has its own tradition, too, and has been another way of drawing attention to Council neglect. As early as 1966 a 'Tidy the Town' campaign was started by the Indian National Association, to draw attention to the Council's failure to provide basic cleaning facilities. Some white residents were furious, seeing it as 'an insult, a farce; an attempt to reflect blame on white people'. But others, recognising that the Council's neglect of the town could have the effect of driving a wedge between black and white, with whites blaming the blacks for the deteriorating conditions, supported the campaign. It was successfully imitated by an Asian resident, who started the Southall Environment Group in 1978 and was elected councillor on the strength of his 'Clean Up Southall' events. In these local residents and children wielded shovels and brushes to clean up the streets and to draw attention once more to the all-encompassing neglect, which included non-removal of domestic rubbish. Protests by mothers with young children, involving stopping traffic on residential roads, have become frequent and have won some response from the Council in terms of plans for 'sleeping policemen' blocks on dangerous roads.

Meanwhile, since 1974, groups of young people have sporadically squatted in empty houses in Southall, both to find somewhere to live for themselves and as a protest against the fact that houses have been left empty for years amidst acute overcrowding and homelessness. Some of these groups came together to form the Southall Campaign for the Single Homeless. In 1980, Ealing Housing Advisory Service, which has campaigned against the Council's neglect of Southall for years, joined with the *Gurdwara* and other community organisations to create a wider community-based body to force the Council to heed Southall.

An Asian town

The systematic neglect by Ealing Borough Council is a long-term issue, not dramatic or explosive by its very nature, but one which has created a smouldering resentment among the people of Southall over the past two decades. With this came the realisation that to the Council, Southall is a kind of black township which is not worth spending money on – a ghetto which it would love to disown. But while the local authority was deliberately neglecting its area of greatest black concentration, the Asians themselves were turning Southall into a self-possessed Asian town.

Southall was one of the first Asian settlements and it became one of the largest. It was close to London and the international airport, making it ideal as a trading centre. The development of Southall as an Asian market-place was also hastened by the arrival of East African Asians expelled from Kenya in 1967 and Uganda in 1972. The majority of these new settlers were Gujerati Hindus, many of whom had a middle-class urban background and had been involved in small businesses. All these factors explain why nowhere else in Britain does an Asian community now have what Southall provides – its own cinemas (two show only Indian films), travel agents, marriage bureaux, banks, grocers, insurance agents, cafes and clothing and jewellery stores. Three Punjabi newspapers are produced in the town and Southall has developed a whole generation of craftsmen. Asians from all over Britain, and even from Europe, look to Southall for their household, social and cultural needs. Asians feel at home there; it is their town in a very real sense. And it was in defence of their town that they took to the streets when the NF and the police invaded it.

The struggle for education

When the first generation realised that by coming to Britain they had not really advanced themselves, and yet could not return home in the near future, they looked for ways to increase the chances for their children in British society. Education seemed to provide the most obvious means. But black parents were soon to find that the educational system was no different from other British institutions – it discriminated against their children. The education of black children became an explosive issue in the 1960s and 1970s.

The labelling of black children: bussing

In 1960, 10 per cent of Southall's children were classed as 'immigrant'; by 1964 the figure was 15 per cent – 1,130 children, of whom the vast majority were Asian, and only 100 West Indian. They were concentrated in certain schools in central Southall. The local education authority report for 1964/5 noted that Beaconsfield Junior and Infants schools had 58 per cent immigrant children.

This concentration had already provoked hostility from some white parents. In June 1963 they complained that the local primary schools were being 'swamped' by Asians. The Council responded by sending a delegation to Edward Boyle, then Minister of Education. When he visited Southall in September to allay white parents' fears, he was greeted by a crowd of BNP members demanding total segregation in schooling. He decided to impose a quota – based purely on colour, not on educational ability – of a maximum of 33 per cent of 'immigrant children' in any one school. The rest were to be 'bussed' out to schools in surrounding areas.

This solution infuriated the hard-line segregationists. In November 1963 300 parents protested against plans at Lady Margaret primary school to introduce a reception class for immigrant children, expressing the view that their children would be contaminated with TB, head lice and 'other immigrant diseases'.

Black parents, by and large, initially approved of bussing. Keen to secure the best possible education for their children, they thought dispersal would mean smaller classes, more individual attention and, above all, integration into the English school system for their children. They were soon to be disillusioned.

By 1967 1,000 children, mainly Asian, were being bussed to schools up to six miles from their homes in order to maintain the quota. Schools in Southall were left with empty places, because they were not taken up by white parents. By 1973, 2,500 children were being bussed, with an additional 400 making their own way to school on public transport. Only black children were bussed. There was no suggestion that white children should travel into Southall to fill the empty places.

The one-way traffic meant that local education became second-class education as the Council neglected educational provision in Southall itself. No new schools were built there, and from 1962 to 1972 (the period when most school-age children were settling) the Council claimed no money at all from central government for the provision of new primary school places. In 1975, when it was estimated that there were 3,000 more primary school children than places in Southall, and at least six new schools were needed, only one was being built.

Through bussing the education of black children became a separate and inferior process. First, every black child was automatically 'assessed'. Asian children were then placed in 'reception' classes, even English-speaking East African Asians. However, European immigrant children were never sent for assessment because, as an education officer explained, 'They would face a culture clash if they had to go to reception classes.'

The reception classes were generally located in prefab huts at the far end of the school grounds. In most schools 12- to-15-year-olds were all in one class with only one teacher to deal with the varying levels of knowledge, language and need. There was very little interaction between reception classes and the main school;

Anti-bussing demonstration

Rockware Glass strike, 1965 (*The Newsline*)

Left: Local MP meets racialists (*Gazette Series*). *Below:* Black youth protest at police harassment (*Gazette Series*)

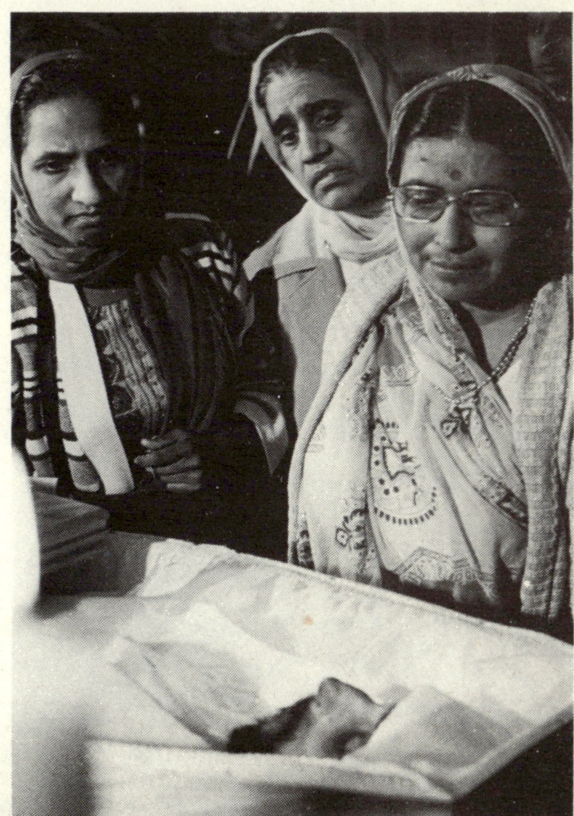

Above: April 23, 1979 (*John Sturrock Network*). *Right:* Southall residents pay their last respects to Blair Peach (*John Sturrock Network*).

Southall mourning march April 28, 1979 (*Laurie Sparham Network*)

Float protesting at trials of 'Southall 342', January 19, 1980 (*Virginia Turbett*)

and what there was was limited in many cases to the remedial department. It was not easy to transfer from reception to normal classes – many children had to wait for over six months, and when they did move, it was usually to the lower streams.

The labelling of black children: ESN

While Asian children were being dumped in reception classes, more and more West Indian parents found their children being placed in the bottom streams of schools or in Educationally Sub-Normal (ESN) schools. In 1972 one-third of pupils at ESN schools in Ealing were black, compared with one-fifth in ordinary schools – and in the latter, West Indian children were over-represented in the bottom streams. West Indian children did not score well on the culture-bound tests and assessments, and were therefore dismissed as stupid. When they rebelled against white definitions of themselves, they were labelled with 'behavioural problems'. A large number were suspended from school – in the 1970s 50 per cent of all school suspensions in Ealing were of West Indian pupils.

Fighting second-class schooling

By the late 1960s, Asian and West Indian parents alike were getting angry about the stereotyping and the second-class education their children were receiving. This anger expressed itself in campaigns against the system of bussing, the racist assessments and the treatment of their children in the schools themselves.

By 1967 some parents were refusing to allow their children to be bussed, and by 1969 the IWA had initiated a sustained campaign against bussing which was to continue into the late 1970s. It was joined by West Indian community representatives and, in 1972, by Ealing Community Relations Council. The campaign emphasised not only the disadvantages the bussed children suffered and the poor education they received, but also the ways in which the segregation of the children created and perpetuated the hostility and racialism which led to attacks on them, both verbal and physical.

The struggle against bussing was conducted by means of lobbying, petitions, surveys and reports. These led to a Race Relations Board investigation in 1975 which concluded that bussing 'may be discriminatory for those who have no educational need for it'. But the Council showed no sign of remedying the situation. Only when local black organisations threatened to prosecute in 1978 did the Council make plans for two new secondary schools in Southall. Meanwhile, according to one estimate, 1,500 black children in Southall were still being bussed out of the town (albeit unofficially, by making their own way on public transport) in 1979.

Parents took up the issues of assessment, suspensions and teachers' attitudes, through their organisations, by making representations to the Council and often by sending deputations straight to the schools involved. Disturbed by the rebellion of black youths, and aware of the support they were getting from black organisations, Ealing Education Authority created the post of Officer for Immigrants (now Assistant Education Officer, Multi-Racial Education) in 1972. In 1973 it set up an Educational Support Team, a Community Education Team and two special pools of teachers, one to teach English as a second language and the other to deal specifically with West Indian students.

In practice, however, these concessions changed little. The teams were at the beck and call of the Education Authority and had no power to alter the structure of education within which they worked. In 1974 a white teacher resigned from Featherstone School, horrified by the 'cultural insensitivity' of the Head in relation to his West Indian pupils. That was at a time when members of the Afro-Caribbean Association, the IWA and the local Pakistani Association were often at the school taking up the numerous complaints of racism made by children. They demanded that any suspension should only be approved by the Education office after consultation with their own organisations. They also sent delegations to the authorities, taking up specific cases, such as Muslim girls who were forced to wear skirts, and general issues, such as assessment and teachers' attitudes. In the same year Ealing CRC set up an inquiry into Featherstone School, after complaints that a letter from the headmaster to local immigrant organisations was racist. Later there were to be inquiries into Villiers School and Belleview ESN School after allegations of maltreatment.

The struggle in the field of education was not confined to activity around the schools. The community also mobilised resources to provide its own education for its children. In 1969 the IWA set up Saturday schools for Asian and West Indian children. Later, the provision was extended to include summer schools, literacy classes for women and counselling for parents.

The struggle against the police

The attitude of the first black settlers – both Asian and West Indian – towards the police was, initially, one of respect. They believed them to be defenders of property, persons and the Queen's peace. But this illusion was also eroded. The first intimation of bias on the part of the police came from their indifference to racist attacks on Asian shops and premises by members of extreme right-wing groups, and their failure to apprehend the culprits. In 1966 community leaders protested about the seeming lack of interest in these crimes. In the next few years more and more protests were made. In 1970, when a gang of skinheads rampaged through Southall attacking Asian youths and smashing windows of Asian shops, the police did nothing. They shrugged their shoulders when black householders reported criminal damage to their homes.

But concern was growing not only about the failure of police to protect black people and their property, but also about their active victimisation. When an Indian bus conductor was insulted by a white passenger who refused to pay her fare, he was the one summonsed for 'insulting behaviour' (and convicted and fined). This not only added to the doubts about the police, but also to those about the impartiality and fairness of the local magistrates' courts.

In 1973 Satnam Kane was accused of stealing £50 from his employers. At the police station he 'confessed' to the theft. It was later discovered that there had been no theft at all – the money had been banked. Kane said he had been forced to confess by threats and physical force. A few months later, Abdul Rashid was arrested at work (at Perivale Gutterman) on suspicion of being an illegal immigrant. He later alleged that he was beaten about the head, stomach, arms and legs and had his genitals pulled at the police station.

There were many other complaints of ill-treatment, racial abuse and the fabrication of evidence by police in their dealings with the black community. By 1973 the number was so large that the leaders of the IWA, the Pakistani Action Committee and the Afro-Caribbean Association asked the Home Secretary to set up an independent inquiry into allegations of police brutality in

Southall. They also complained that the Director of Public Prosecutions had taken no action in cases of obvious police perjury in court.

Meanwhile, Ealing CRC initiated an inquiry from Stanislaus Pullé. He took 50 cases, discarded those where he considered the complainant had previously had 'anti-police' attitudes and then took 12 of those remaining to investigate in depth. The report came out in November 1973, and substantiated the complaints. 'There is a *prima facie* case against the police on charges of brutality and partial conduct against the immigrant community in Ealing.'

So strong was the condemnation that attempts were made to suppress the report. Meanwhile, a member of the CRC secretly handed it over to the police before publication, and subsequently there were complaints that the police tried to seek out some of those who had given evidence against them. But eventually the report was released, and Ealing Trades Council condemned the police prejudice, insults and criminal behaviour and the complicity of magistrates that were revealed.

In response to the Pullé Report, Ealing CRC set up a police liaison committee in 1974. From the start, however, it was clear that the police were more interested in promoting their public image than listening seriously to the complaints against them. Community leaders, presenting individual cases of harassment, were told, 'We can't do anything about individual cases'; yet if they attempted to raise the question of police attitudes and harassment in general, they were then asked to be more specific. The respect and dignity the black community demanded was never forthcoming. The liaison committee stumbled along for a year or so, was suspended and restored, only to collapse finally after the events of April 23, 1979. But by then, the image of the police among the black community resembled far more that of their colonial experience than the idealised British bobby. 'Monday's police terrorism', said the local *Punjab Times* (1.5.79), 'has convinced people that Southall has been reduced to the status of a British Imperial Colony from that of a town of free citizens.'

The struggle against controls

The organisations set up by the new arrivals in the late 1950s had a lot to do, helping countrymen to find accommodation and fill out tax returns and other forms and sorting out money, work and language problems. But by 1961 it was evident that a whole new dimension was to be added to their work by the impending immigration legislation.

In January 1961 a Home Office official stated: 'The Government refuses to contemplate legislation which might restrict the historic right of every British subject, regardless of race and colour, freely to enter and stay in the UK.' But despite this and similar declarations, it was clear by the middle of the year that restrictions were to be introduced. When the Commonwealth Immigrants Bill was published, the IWA mounted a campaign. It held a number of public meetings and encouraged broad-based opposition to immigration control. The first meeting was addressed by Fenner Brockway MP, Claudia Jones, of the *West Indian Gazette*, Mahmood Hashmi, editor of *Mashriq*, and Vishnu Sharma, of the IWA.

But the Bill became law and immigration control became a reality. It was soon taken for granted by most white Britons, but it gravely affected the black communities in their family lives. Nearly every family had relatives in the Indian subcontinent or the West Indies planning to come at some stage and join the family here. Nearly every family had friends wanting to come and see how things were before deciding whether to come and settle too. Marriages had to be organised, visits made. All this became extremely difficult for those without a British passport, and it meant more work for the organisations. The IWA set up an advisory service for immigrants.

But controls were to get a lot worse. Under the 1965 White Paper, entry vouchers (needed for settlement for non-UK passport holders) were stopped for unskilled workers. The IWA campaigned strongly against this move. It joined the Campaign Against Racial Discrimination in the same year, and in 1967 both joined with the West Indian Standing Conference to form the Joint Council for the Welfare of Immigrants, whose first meeting was held in the Dominion Cinema.

The 1968 Commonwealth Immigrants Act removed the right of black UK passport holders to enter Britain. Then, the 1971 Act, the most draconian, took away the right of entry for settlement of Commonwealth citizens with work vouchers. Thenceforth, workers from Commonwealth countries were all subject to immigration control, and were here on sufferance only, with no right to stay, unless they were 'patrial' – which in practice tended to mean 'white'. The 1971 Act provoked fury from black organisations. In spite of another vigorous campaign, it had been passed. But one battle was won. Initially, when the Act came into force in January 1973, it was applied retrospectively. In protest, the IWA and local West Indian organisations withdrew representation from all statutory bodies, including Ealing CRC. This kind of pressure finally led to the dismantling of all retrospective elements in the Act.

However, the Act, the Rules made under it, and judicial decisions since 1973 have made the practice of immigration control a nightmare, not only for visitors and for dependants coming to join their fathers and husbands after years of separation but also for people already settled here. After waiting for years for entry permits, wives and children are subjected to degrading treatment, not only verbal, but physical (X-rays and medical examinations), to determine their age, state of health and relationship to their sponsor. Visits often end with an entry refusal at Heathrow, accompanied by accusations of fraud, prolonged examinations and detention. The police (and particularly the Special Branch), brought in more and more to enforce the Act, have powers of detention and questioning which mean that anyone with a black skin can be detained on suspicion and held indefinitely, without trial. People who think they have been lawfully settled here for years are detained and held to be 'illegal' on the strength of something said, or not said, to the immigration officer when they arrived. The right of habeas corpus, whereby unlawful detention can be challenged, has been so eroded that it no longer affords protection for immigrants.

If the tightening of the screw of immigration control – by law and practice – before and since 1971 was designed to demoralise and frighten the black communities into packing their bags and leaving, it has not worked. Rather, the effect has been to draw them closer together to fight, using both conventional channels and the resources of the community. The IWA has pressed on, both with its work of advising and helping those in difficulties with the law and with its campaigning work. In 1976, and again in 1979, with other groups it organised pickets at Heathrow and Harmondsworth to protest against practices like the virginity testing of Asian women and against prolonged detention of suspected 'illegals'. No one in Southall is likely to be bullied or 'induced' into going home – Southall is their home.

Race and party politics

Traditionally, Southall was a Labour stronghold, a working-class area whose members had come from Wales, Ireland and northern England for work on the railways and in the foundries and factories. And it was the working class which bore the social costs of immigration – the additional stress of already overstretched, run-down, scarce amenities in an overcrowded area – while the factory owners and the national economy took the profit. So, with local and central government alike simply ignoring the increased needs of the community as a whole, it is not surprising that the white working class of the town became more susceptible to racialist ideas to explain away the material problems.

Neither the local Council nor the local MP did anything to correct the idea that the physical problems of the town were the immigrants' fault; indeed we have seen how, over the housing issue, the Council encouraged it by giving way to racialists' demands. The Labour MP, George Pargiter, opposed the first Act to restrict coloured immigration in 1962. But in 1963 – the year of the Southall Residents' Association formation and of the demands for segregated education in his constituency – he only abstained on the review of the Act. By January 1964, with a general election in sight, he was urging a 'complete ban on immigration to Southall'.

Angered by Labour's attitude locally and nationally, the IWA decided to make a start in British party politics, by putting up its own candidate for the local elections. But the SRA – which had been continually urging the Council to get tough on overcrowding and complaining to it and to Pargiter about 'prostitution and vice' in the Northcote area – threatened to put up its own candidate in opposition. The IWA withdrew, instead advising its members to vote Labour, in the absence of anything better.

From the BNP to the NF

In the 1964 general election neither of the main parties in Southall made an issue of race, as occurred, for example, in Smethwick. This was left to the British National Party (BNP), whose candidate, John Bean, held nine public meetings exclusively on immigration. His platform was a ban on further coloured immigration, and no National Assistance for unemployed immigrants unless they applied for repatriation. Stickers appeared throughout the town saying 'Stop Southall becoming a Black Slum – Vote Bean'. Once again the IWA threw its weight behind the Labour Party. By now there were an estimated 6,300 Asians and West Indians in Southall, of whom two-thirds were single men. The local Labour Party printed leaflets in Urdu and Punjabi, and the IWA helped to distribute them, as well as canvassing for Labour at the weekly film show.

The BNP polled 9.1 per cent of the vote – its highest ever in a general election. Pargiter, who retained his seat by a very reduced margin, promptly forgot about the black vote that had helped him save it. He neglected to invite a single black person to his victory celebrations. In an interview with the *New Statesman* he said, 'I feel that Sikh parents should encourage their children to give up their turbans, their religion and their dietary laws. If they refuse to integrate, then we must be tough. They should be told that they would be the first to go if there was unemployment.' Pargiter had moved a long way in two short years.

For the extreme right organisations, 1964 had been a good year. But as the mainstream parties absorbed some of their ideas, and immigration control became taken for granted – and as the racial balance of the town's population changed – the popularity of the extreme right in Southall waned. The SRA continued to put pressure on estate agents not to sell to black families, and to lobby the MP to halt immigration. In 1966 some of its founder members joined the Racial Preservation Society (RPS), and thereafter there was close liaison between the two groups. The SRA also demanded that the Federation of Ealing Residents' Associations – to which it was affiliated – sever its links with the newly-formed Ealing International Friendship Committee. But by 1966 many whites – those who could afford to – had moved out to surrounding areas (Hayes, Harlington, Northolt and Greenford) and nearly one quarter of Central Southall's residents were black.

This meant a loss of support for the BNP too. Its vote in the 1966 general election was down to 7.4 per cent. The leadership then decided to merge with the Greater Britain Movement, headed by neo-Nazi John Tyndall. But this party was too extreme for many: Tyndall himself had just received a six-month prison sentence for possessing arms and ammunition. The merger caused a split, with many members resigning, some of whom joined other racialists in

1967 to form the National Front, which soon had a working relationship with the SRA and RPS.

Until 1967 local workplaces had been relatively free of active racialist organisations. The local unions, like the Labour Council, had by and large simply ignored the problems of their black members. However, during the years of 'stop-go' economic policy and fading prosperity, the SRA (and later the NF) began to organise in the factories around Southall. In 1967 (the same year that the TUC came out against proposals to protect black workers from discrimination by legislation) Greenford TGWU sent a motion to Ealing Trades Council calling for a ban on immigration – the SRA was suspected of being behind it. The motion was rejected, but by March 1968 the SRA had organised sufficiently to hold two union meetings chaired by their local candidate, John Cripps. This resulted in a petition to the TUC, circulated in nine local factories, calling for a ban on immigration and the 'protection of native workers'.

By establishing footholds in the unions, the racialist groups were ready to take advantage of Enoch Powell's 'Rivers of Blood' speech in April 1968. A few days after it, two SRA councillors (expelled from the Labour Party on the council house residence qualification issue in 1965), acting in their capacity as senior shop stewards at AEC, led a 'spontaneous' march in support of Powell. A meeting in the White Hart, Southall, in support of Powell was attended by representatives of workers from British Oxygen, AEC, a section of London Transport, Heathrow Airport, EMI, Allied Iron Foundries, Brittanic Cables, Lyons and Acrow Engineers.

Due to Southall TGWU, which publicly condemned this move and passed resolutions against racialism, and to the attitude of the Trades Council, the local racialist movement in the unions subsided. However, in October 1969 it still had sufficient influence to bring out 200 people on a 'white solidarity' march, organised by the NF and the SRA, with the slogan of 'Send 'em Back'. The events of 1968/9 had shown that as long as black workers were at the bottom of the pile, and trade unions generally indifferent to them, racialist ideas could be spread among the white workforce.

The local Tories also supported Powell, thereby giving an official seal of approval to racial hysteria. 1969/70 saw an epidemic of racial violence in Southall – lightheartedly referred to as 'Paki-bashing' – further encouraged by literature put out by the NF, the SRA and the RPS. But in 1970 the NF polled only 4.4 per cent of Southall's vote in the general election. The days of electoral popularity were over for the extreme right in Southall. The white exodus was continuing, as was the arrival of more dependants of the original black settlers, as well as some East African Asians. The following year, 1971, the population of the two Central Southall wards was 49 per cent Asian/West Indian. From then until 1979 there was no local electoral activity by the extreme right. The organisations followed their members out – to Uxbridge, Hayes, Greenford and Feltham.

In 1972, when Amin expelled British passport-holding Asians from Uganda, the media and the politicians once again sensationalised race and immigration. As reporters depicted Southall as 'Little India' (an apparently horrifying idea!), the local Tories seized on the occasion to call for a halt on all primary immigration (a year after the 1971 Act which, in effect, had done just that). The Labour Leader of the Council demanded that the Ugandan Asians be induced to settle anywhere but Southall,* and, not to be outdone, Sidney Bidwell, the successor to Pargiter as Labour MP, remarked that the town 'could not take any more immigrants'. The organised extreme right was not there, in large numbers, to fan the flames. There were, however, continual racialist protests: for example, a few ratepayers, led by the secretary of the local Monday Club, applied for a reduction in rates because 'population changes in the area have caused a deterioration in amenities' (which, ironically, was true, since the 'blacker' Southall became, the less the Council spent on it). In December local residents received hoax letters from unidentified right-wing groups telling them that up to ten Ugandan Asian families were to be billeted on each of them. But the racialists expended their electoral effort elsewhere, where there were more disgruntled white voters. The West Middlesex Monday Club supported the NF in a by-election in Uxbridge. They were ordered to disband, but received sympathy from Southall's Tory candidate, who said he knew how they felt. The following year the NF took 11.5 per cent of the vote in Feltham & Heston and 8.5 per cent in Hayes and Harlington. But there was no NF candidate in Southall.

---

*The government designated Southall a 'red' area, i.e., one where Ugandan Asians should not settle.

Racial attacks continued sporadically throughout the 1970s, but mainly in the peripheral areas, such as Greenford and Northolt, where black families had been housed on all-white estates. The right impinged less on the black community as a whole as a threat to daily well-being, compared with the police, the Housing Department and the Home Office.

Tory racism unleashed

In May 1978, the Council changed hands – for the first time in many years Ealing was controlled by the Tories. A new era was ushered in. Margaret Thatcher was not yet in power as Prime Minister, but her philosophy and politics on race, her 'swamping the culture' speech, was to find resonance at a local level in Tory councils long before May 1979. Thatcherism was rife in Ealing. The first hint came after a Rock Against Racism carnival in a local park during the summer of 1978. It was a good-natured and peaceful affair, featuring Misty and the Ruts, a local punk band; but much to RAR's fury the Council banned future carnivals there.

Then, in the autumn, the General Purposes Committee agreed to let the NF book a room at Ealing Town Hall for a meeting. The decision had to be confirmed by the Council, which until then had had a policy of not letting to fascist groups. A rowdy meeting with a large Southall delegation ensured that the booking did not go ahead. But a few months later the same Council accepted a NF booking for April 23 – in the very centre of Southall.

Local individuals and groups were galvanised into action – lobbying and campaigning to stop the meeting. On April 10 the IWA held an emergency meeting to draw up plans; on April 11 ECRC and the IWA appealed to the Conservative Leader of the Council to change the decision. On the same day a meeting of over 80 representatives, convened by the IWA, decided to set up a coordinating committee and issued a leaflet, which included a petition calling on the Council to cancel the meeting, notice of a protest march on April 22, a call for a half-day strike on April 23 and plans for a peaceful sit-down outside the Town Hall from 5pm on that day. On April 13 ECRC wrote to all Ealing Councillors urging them to call on the Leader to withdraw permission to the NF. On April 17 local solicitors wrote on behalf of the IWA to the Town Clerk asking for a reversal of the decision, and if this was not forthcoming that 100 members of the IWA be allowed to attend the meeting. On the same day members of the coordinating committee met the local police Community Liaison Officer and Scotland Yard representatives who agreed to a peaceful sit-down protest. On April 18 ECRC sent telegrams to the Prime Minister, the Home Secretary and the Chairman of the Commission for Racial Equality, saying that they feared violence. On April 19 members of the coordinating committee had an interview with the Home Secretary who agreed to speak to Metropolitan Police Commissioner McNee about keeping April 23 peaceful. But all to no avail.

4 Growing up black in Britain

The black community of Southall, had, as we have shown, fought against racism all along the line. The methods it chose for its struggle were influenced by the relationships and traditions its members brought with them, albeit adapted to British realities. In the main this had meant first creating their own organisations and later involved negotiating (whether via an elder, a delegation or a community petition) with the system. The local authority, the schools, the Home Office, the police, all had to be liaised with so as to save themselves and especially their children from the worst aspects of a second-class status. The first generation of Southall's black settlers had a dual consciousness and a double burden. For whilst striving here to fulfil their duties to their family, they also had responsibilities to their extended family back home. Whilst living in the British present, they also had a vision of the future – a return home.

For their children there was no dual consciousness, no 'home' where they belonged. There was nothing with which they could transmute the racism they encountered. For those who had been born or brought up and educated in Britain, racism was not just in the systems of society that decided their life chances, but something tangible that they faced every day, at school and on the streets of Southall. They were forced to adopt a different form of struggle from that of their parents. Below we trace the way *their* experience of racism informed *their* resistance.

At school

The Asian children who were bussed to school had long journeys, often leaving home at 7.30am to travel out of familiar surroundings to places that were strange and often hostile. Their parents, denied the right to choose where their children should be educated, did not know the schools well, far away as they were, and the schools' contact with them was minimal. As one local put it, 'They go as outsiders, they stay as outsiders and they come back as outsiders.'

At school the children were faced with hostility from children in the main school, who regarded them as inferiors and outsiders. (In one school reception classes were called 'nut hospitals'.) In many cases this resulted in Asian children wanting to stay in reception classes or the bottom streams because their lives were made a misery if they moved up – A and B streams were for whites only. They could not stay to join in after-school activities because of the long journey home. They did not know the names of the bullies from other classes so they could never complain. All this intensified the isolation that bussing and reception classes had begun.

West Indian children also suffered at the hands of the teachers. They were told that they had 'unrealistic aspirations', that they were 'cheeky', that they had a 'chip on their shoulder'. As one West Indian recalls: 'They thought we were backward and took us right back to scratch, so of course we got bored, lost interest. We couldn't relate to their way of teaching; they couldn't relate to what we wanted to learn ... Teachers not only think you're stupid, but the sort of things they teach you make you believe you're stupid. I think some of them are born racialists.' And Asian children, too, became increasingly aware of the inappropriateness and racial bias of their education. As a pupil at Villiers High School put it: 'I remember thinking when I was younger that maybe, somehow, my language – the language of my parents – isn't a real language ... All our history is from a British point of view. We're taught that Robert Clive was a hero and how the British introduced the railway and democracy to India .. but we're never told how Indian industry was smashed and replaced by British industry ... what they are saying all the time is that white is right. So we grow up with English nicknames and no self respect.'

The majority of black children were expected to take CSEs rather than O levels. There were cases of parents, who insisted on their children doing O levedls, having to pay for private tuition and the exam itself.

Racial fights in and outside school were a common feature of life for many Asian children. A former student of Dormers Wells school describes the situation: 'Featherstone was the first secondary school to have a large proportion of Asian children. Our parents felt it would be better if we went to Dormers Wells, where there were not many Asians. It was a white-dominated area. There were far more white kids than Asians and very few West Indians. There were racial fights every day – even going through the corridors you were in danger of attack. The teachers would lock their rooms and just carry on teaching. They didn't want to get involved. Featherstone was by then about 40 per cent Asian, so the older kids there would come to Dormers Wells to escort us, to be there at lunchtime and breaks. Outside the school the violence would continue and people would come out of their houses to support the white kids. White mothers taking their children to a primary school further down the road didn't want to pass our gates because of the daily fights. At one stage they put a panda car outside the school gates.' The attacks decreased as the number of Asians in the school grew and their ability to fight back increased.

For the bussed children the problems were the same. The long waits they had for the transport made them more vulnerable to attack – at one school teachers used to guard the Asian children waiting for the buses. Sometimes it used to be a struggle even to get the buses to stop, and London Transport had to be alerted. Two schools used to send the children home half an hour early each day to try to get over the problem – which meant that they missed five periods of school each week. Building on the escort system they had created at Dormers Wells school, Asian pupils would go over to Acton schools to protect the bussed children.

Most of the fights were not publicised, but some did come to the notice of the press. In 1968, after Enoch Powell's 'Rivers of Blood' speech, a gang of white youths armed with iron bars appeared outside a Southall school and beat up Asian boys. In 1973 13-year-old Durgesh Patel was attacked by youths near Vincent Secondary School in Eastcott Lane. In 1974 Abdul Malik was killed in Greenford Broadway, while waiting for the bus back to Southall, in an inter-school fight between 15-year-old pupils.

The youths encountered racism in other areas too. There were struggles over entry into the few clubs of Southall; there was harassment by the police in their meeting places and on the street, and there were attacks from white racialist gangs.

In the early 1960s it was the West Indian youth who bore the brunt of this. 'No blacks were allowed at either Parkview youth club or at the White Hart club in Southall. We started walking into the White Hart club; there'd always be a fight and the police would wait outside and arrest West Indians. But in the end, as some of the white youths moved away the management gave in and the club was given to the West Indians to run. But the police harassed it every night. They'd come in anytime, raiding for drugs or just barging in and picking up people. There were lots of fights with the police.' The only alternative was the Featherstone youth club (formerly Dovetail). It was run by a West Indian, and there the youth could learn about African culture and started organising theatre, music and dance groups.

West Indian dances at the Dominion Cinema attracted a large police presence and West Indians who responded to the racist goading as they left, were often picked up and sometimes beaten. During the 1960s there were many reports of youths being arrested, taken to Southall police station and beaten up. One youth reported having had his head pushed down a lavatory, others alleged brutality and total disregard of basic rights.

And when a West Indian was attacked, police action was not forthcoming. On May 30, 1970, Reginald Passey, an 18-year-old West Indian, was shot at by a white boy. A week later West Indians from the Oasis youth club (where Reginald was a member) held a demonstration outside Acton police station to protest at police inaction. This resulted in almost complete breakdown of relations between the club and the police.

The white clubs were not for Asian youth either, but they did have the Indian Youth Club. Started in 1966 as a recreational centre, it provided a meeting place. It was not until the 1970s that it extended its activities, taking youth to see workplaces and different parts of London, inviting outside speakers, and discussing school experiences and beginning to organise the youth more coherently.

At first, there was little interaction between West Indian and Asian youth; they kept separate and saw little in common between their experiences and struggles. 'Asians spoke a different language, had a different culture. They couldn't relate to us because in the colonial system the Asians were put above the black', explained a West Indian youth. An Asian youth saw it differently: 'Some West Indians even sided with the whites against us in school fights.'

It was in the late 1960s, in the wake of Powell's speeches, that the 'Paki-bashing' era hit Southall and, ironically, provided the catalyst for uniting the black youth. Gangs of white youths roamed the streets on the look out for blacks. The police did nothing. But if a West Indian or Asian got involved they were liable to arrest. In 1969 there were several fights in Southall between black and white youth. Then, in 1970, on the day of the IWA elections, about 150 skinheads came into Southall and there was a battle on the main street – people were attacked with bottles and beaten up. At that point the West Indian youth were forced to take sides, and from then on came together with the Asian youth for protection against such attacks. The noticeable lack of police assistance or even presence during this incident was for some Asian youth the beginning of disillusionment with the police.

This disillusionment coincided with the fact that the Asian youth had their first 'hangout', a local café in the centre of Southall, and this meeting place, just like the West Indian clubs, was subject to police raids. 'If anything happened anywhere in Southall the police would converge on the café. It would be cordoned off by panda cars – about 15 officers per visit, about three times a week. Gradually the harassment grew and we noticed the racial dimension. In any incident it seemed that the black would be worse off, the black person would be picked up, not the whites.' The police also split up groups of children on their way home from school. 'We'd walk in groups of seven or so as protection and we'd be nicked for obstruction if we didn't split up. Most of us got pulled in at some point. There were a lot of racial attacks, but no whites were charged, so in the end they weren't even reported.'

Raids on black centres and meeting places became even more frequent during the 1970s. In 1972 the George pub, where many West Indians had their lunch, was raided. Plainclothes police came in and smashed things up and several West Indian youths were beaten up in the process. Six months later police carried out a massive raid on the Burton Centre, a meeting place for black youth from Acton, Southall and Brent. At the Swan pub in Southall, Asians were beaten up by white thugs on a number of occasions. When the police arrived (called by the landlord) they would watch the fights and then arrest the Asians. In 1974, a year after the Pullé Report, there was so much disquiet in the community over the serious conflict arising from the police pursuit of suspected persons into youth clubs and the use of police dogs that, as we have already reported, the police and ECRC met to draft proposals for a police liaison committee.

The police agreed not to take dogs into clubs and to liaise on a regular basis (until then cricket matches had been the extent of police-community involvement). Representatives of local clubs, invited to a liaison committee meeting, agreed that the police should visit their premises in an attempt at reducing the conflict. In June 1975, for example, police met West Indians at the Nocta club – where they were heavily criticised for their treatment of black people. A few months later, during an incident at the Co-op Hall the police arrived with dogs. Immediately the level of youth representation at the liaison committee dropped.

A West Indian youth recalls relations with the police: 'There was nowhere to go. We were picked up by the police – they'd have these pre-Christmas swoops, rounding up the kids, as many as possible, to have them in prison over Christmas. Most West Indian youths had spells in prison. There were vicious police then – the youth started fighting back. There was one particular copper, called "Blue Eyes", who harassed the youth, beating them up, till the youths got him and beat him. He left Southall for a couple of years, then came back wanting revenge and was even worse. He got beaten again, and was moved from Southall. But the funny thing was, the raid on Peoples Unite a few weeks before April 23rd, old "Blue Eyes" was leading it. He was in plainclothes. So they must have moved him back for that.'

Murder in Southall

In 1976 racialism in the country reached another high. The national media fuelled anti-immigrant sentiment with its wide publicity for the misleading Hawley report on dependants, its racist debates on immigration and Powellite propaganda that white Britain was about to be swamped by an endless flow of dependants from the New Commonwealth. The story of a

Malawian Asian family housed in a four-star hotel got front page treatment by the media. As always, when such publicity is given, there was a corresponding increase in racial attacks on black people, in particular on Asians, all over the country. Black bookshops and centres and places of worship were attacked in the Southall area, as in the rest of the country. In north-east London two black students were murdered on the streets. Then, on Friday, June 4, 1976, Gurdip Singh Chaggar was attacked by a group of white youths and stabbed to death in Southall.

The murder of Chaggar, in the midst of a large and strong Asian community, was a shock to all. The fact that it had taken place outside the Dominion Cinema, a symbol of Asian self-reliance and security, gave the death an added significance. News of the murder sped through the town the following morning. By Saturday afternoon groups of angry Asian youths were collecting in the area, and in the evening outbreaks of spontaneous violence occurred – cans and stones were thrown at cars. At first the police were unprepared and outnumbered, but by 8pm they had reinforcements and began systematically to stop and search Asians, many of whom were charged with carrying offensive weapons and obstruction. This strengthened the feeling that the police were more concerned with policing the Asian community than with arresting those responsible for the murder. The youth asked the IWA to close the Dominion Cinema that evening and the next day as a mark of respect for Chaggar. They made similar requests to shops, restaurants and two other Asian cinemas in the area. The IWA asked for extra police, both to protect Asians in Southall from whites and to restrain the agitated community.

'We shall fight like lions'

The IWA had a meeting on fascism planned for the Sunday and this went ahead. Those on the platform responded to the youths' demand for action by presenting a resolution to the meeting which abstracted the event in Southall into a generalised condemnation of media and politicians: 'The present situation is the direct result of the climate of racial hysteria created by the misleading and inflammatory propaganda carried out by the NF and Mr E. Powell against the immigrants. The conference is further of the opinion that the governing political parties and the media of the country are equally to blame for the present situation.'

But the youth had no time for resolutions, nor for reliance on the goodwill of politicians. Nothing had come out of them in the past. Something more had to be done; there had to be immediate action and the only way was for them to organise themselves. After the meeting an impromptu demonstration was planned to march on Southall police station to 'demand protection from racial attacks'. There was no trouble until a car pulled up outside the Dominion and a white man, wielding a pickaxe handle, shouted 'You black bastards'. Then, as the youth marched to the police station, a police van window was smashed and cans and stones were thrown at cars and shops. The white community as a whole had been identified as the enemy – the youth were wild with anger. One Asian was arrested and when the youth arrived at the police station they found it barricaded. So they staged a 'sit down' outside. The youth were in command, it was they who now made the speeches. 'We shall fight like lions'* was the rallying call. After half an hour the police tried to disperse them by force and arrested another youth. The demonstrators then demanded the unconditional release of both those arrested. Eventually they were let go, one unconditionally and one on bail (though the latter was not realised at the time).

On Sunday evening another meeting was held by the youth, in the Century Cinema. Here, disaffected with the IWA and other organisations which had not been prepared to act in their defence, they differentiated themselves from their elders. It was agreed not to do anything to provoke a confrontation with the police and that there should not be indiscriminate attacks on whites, but plans were made to organise self-defence units. This meeting laid the basis for the Southall Youth Movement.

That same evening, from 8pm onwards, the police set up road blocks on four main roads in and around Southall and cars were stopped and searched. Many Asians reported that it was their cars, not those of white people, that got the attention. Callaghan, then Home Secretary, responded to the Asian leaders' appeal to speak out in support of ethnic minorities by condemning race riots instead, adding that the government would continue to oppose racialism in any form: 'I urge everyone not to allow passion to destroy our reputation as a tolerant, cohesive and unified

---

*The lion being the Sikh symbol of bravery.

society.' Press coverage of the events concentrated on the sensational – 'race riots', the violence of the youth and so on. The press also played up the differences between the militant youth and the older members of the community, interpreting it as a generation gap of massive proportions. But the criticisms of the adults were in their role as leaders, not as adults. The difference was in the strategies – the youth rejected the attitude of 'keeping a low profile', they refused to take things lying down. In fact, many of the parents sympathised with the more militant tactics adopted by their children to express their grievances.

The massive and militant response by the youth to the murder of Chaggar included a rejection of the traditional politics of Southall. The IWA leaders, whom the youth had known and watched since their childhood, now seemed to be standing in the way of what the youth felt had to be done. By challenging the traditional political form, the youth were also articulating their need to organise in terms of British realities, as opposed to the IWA which was based and organised around politics which emanated from the Indian subcontinent.

It was not only the IWA which at this time was by-passed by the youth. From 1971 Southall had seen the growth of government-funded community-based 'self-help' projects. Some community workers, sensing the growing rift between the youth and the traditional organisations and statutory agencies, set up the National Association of Indian Youth (NAIY) 'to involve the community from inside and stimulate them to take action to achieve their own objectives'. Scope Southall was also set up, in 1973, as 'an independent local project', 'free from the control of the local authority, community organisations and community relations council, but still part of the community' with projects for youth, the unemployed, the elderly, young wives, pre-school children, and so on.

Many of the youth had gravitated to these burgeoning self-help projects. But by 1976, seeing through their claims to be a solution for the community, the youth recognised them for what they were – palliatives which did not change the fundamental structures of power relationships. And try though the Manpower Services Commission did, after 1976, to control the militant youth by pouring large funds into Southall, via ECRC, NAIY and Scope, it could not buy off their rebellion. The youths gained know-how from working in these projects and put it to use in forming their own organisations to meet their own self-defined needs. The most important independent organisations that developed were Southall Youth Movement (started by Asians) and Peoples Unite (started by young West Indians).

The death of Chaggar may have been the incident that spurred the Asian youth into organising themselves, but the basis of their militancy was the racism that they experienced at school, in the streets and in the search for jobs. 'Most of the kids who leave school don't go to college and they won't find a job. They'll be on the streets with their culture pounded out of them', said an Asian youth. At first the youth had organised around their Punjabi identity, making the use of their language, which some of them had forgotten, a symbol of their non-whiteness and the stand they were taking. But with Chaggar's death the cultural reaction took on a much more political form and the links built up during their school days in order to protect themselves gave them a political base.

Southall Youth Movement

The SYM gained a following in local schools and youth clubs. Apart from physically keeping racism off the streets of Southall – it picketed the Hambrough Tavern in 1978 because it refused to serve blacks, and demonstrated against Powell when he spoke locally – its main concern was the lack of youth provision in the Borough. In 1977 SYM squatted a building and began converting it to its own use. This acquisition of premises was a major break through – space and basic facilities could be provided for various projects, the aim being to encourage genuine self-help. 'The weight-lifting club which we started is now autonomous. It came from nothing, but now it's much bigger, does its own fundraising work and so on. We acted as a catalyst by providing the initial impetus and facility. This is our function.' Some nights each week SYM works with other youth centres. Its aim is to provide sports, recreational and welfare facilities, and advice on housing and employment problems.

'One of the greatest achievements', said one SYM member, 'is that it has bridged the gap between Asian and West Indian youngsters and that it works closely with Peoples Unite.' Their common experiences of living in a racist society has brought them together to deal with the problems that black youth are faced with locally and nationally. As the largest organised youth group in Southall, the SYM made plans for protesting on April 23. Having seen the petition to cancel the NF's meeting fail, and all appeals to politicians fall on deaf ears, SYM planned a picket near the Town Hall on the afternoon of the NF's meeting. This was communicated to the police who appeared to find it acceptable; even on the day itself, the community policeman, Gosse, gave the youth permission to advance towards the Town Hall. It was as the SYM youth made their way to their picket that the massive police onslaught began in earnest.

In the Punjabi press there was nothing but praise for the resistance of Asian youth on that day. 'They were struggling for us and for the cause of order, peace and good race relations; for organising and leading us in this cause they deserve our respect ... Alongside other whites and blacks they were fighting against the followers of Hitler.' (*Des Perdes* 4/5/79) Both this paper and *Sandesh* saw the resistance in Southall as completely justified in terms of self-defence – 'as a wounded snake stings back', 'If anyone tries to damage our self-respect without any reason then we will fight back.' And the *Punjab Times* (15/5/79) strongly criticised the mass media for dwelling on particular situations which could demonstrate the trouble-making and provocative aspects of Asian youth involvement. *Des Perdes,* in an unusually firm message, showed just how much impact the militancy in Southall had had on the whole community: 'We won't accept to live like second-class citizens and forego our rights. It is natural for us to feel worried and concerned when Special Patrol Group policemen go around sniffing human blood to protect the NF.'

Peoples Unite

'I left school with a number of "O" levels. I went to the careers office and was told to go to Hoovers as a labourer and if I was lucky I might learn a trade after a time', a West Indian youth recalls. 'They don't educate the children, they just provide fodder for the factories', one parent put it bitterly. 'The new generation who were born here is lost', explained one of the founders of Peoples Unite.

The rising number of black unemployed, their disenchantment with the educational system and the racism they encountered on a daily basis were all factors contributing to the setting up of Peoples Unite Education and Creative Arts Centre by a group of West Indian youths and some local community workers in 1978.

But its roots were further back, in the development of the reggae group Misty. In the early 1970s Misty played in youth clubs and became very popular. But it wanted more than that – it wanted to put its music to use for the people, West Indian and Asian. So started the search for a permanent place where the youth could have full control and the pride of building something up without grants. Out of this grew Peoples Unite, the beginnings of the alternative community centre, and its musicians' co-op, People Unite, consisting of Misty, the Enchanters, Bongo Danny and Reality (and later the Ruts).

People Unite gradually got itself off the ground. 'We were trying to be self-supporting; we bought our own PA system from our earnings and built up equipment over a long period. We bought our own trucks and vans.' As one member of Misty put it: 'We chose to use our music and our position for the strength and independence of our people. To be independent. We knew little about production and had little money, but our reasons were right.' They also had contact with other political groups, working closely with Rock Against Racism in 1977 and 1978.

Meanwhile, the wider project, Peoples Unite, encountered a setback. Its members had started work on some premises owned by the Middlesex Housing Association. Then the Association changed its mind, deciding to use the premises as flats instead, and threw them out. But eventually, Peoples Unite moved into 6 Parkview Road, owned by Ealing Social Services and due for demolition in 1985, and fixed it up. That was in 1978.

6 Parkview incorporated a general drop-in centre and the musicians' co-op. Classes in literacy, numeracy, black history, drama and dance were set up. Arranged jointly with SYM, tuition in carpentry and mechanics were also available. Girls Unite also used the premises, providing a meeting place for women, black studies and advice, and with plans for a creche and a women's resource centre.

Peoples Unite never applied for grants, believing that only by being independent could it keep control over its own existence, activities and future. At one time, the ECRC offered to pay some wages. Some members accepted these for a time, but they soon found that 'through that they tried to infiltrate us, buy us'.

In the weeks leading up to April 23, Peoples Unite was singled out for attention by the local police. Five weeks before, they carried out a heavy and unnecessary raid on the centre on the pretext of searching for stolen property – nothing was found. People Unite's sax player was arrested for 'theft' at about the same time (later he was acquitted in court). Two weeks before April 23, two youths were picked up on their way back to Parkview after buying some paint. The police released them after a picket of the police station. But the police told them: 'We know you bastards at no. 6 and we're going to get you.'

That is exactly what happened on April 23.

After the police smashed up everything inside 6 Parkview on April 23, the building itself was demolished by Ealing Borough Council. Since then, Peoples Unite has not been able to re-open in Southall. Most of its founder members have moved their activities to Ealing. So West Indian and Asian youths lost an important base.

5 Postscript

If the death of Gurdip Chaggar had galvanised the youth of Southall, the tragic and shocking events of April 23, 1979, succeeded in uniting the whole community in its outrage against the police, and through them the racism of the state. Nearly every black family in Southall had at least one member who was on the streets that day, who had witnessed mass arrests, followed by 'justice' being meted out on the streets by thousands of police who ran amok. The unbounded anger that was felt throughout the community was reflected in the local Punjabi press: 'Monday's police terrorism has convinced people that Southall has been reduced to the status of a British Imperial Colony, from that of a town of free citizens' (*Punjab Times*, 1.5.79). *Des Perdes* (4.5.79) drew another parallel with colonial occupation, equating the police behaviour with the Jallian-Wala Bagh holocaust of April 1919 in Amritsar (Punjab), in which hundreds of men, women and children attending a peaceful protest meeting were gunned down by the British army.

Immediately, the anger of the community focussed on the death of Blair Peach, who had been murdered defending their town. His death became the symbol of their outrage, it affected the black community as much as if he had been one of their sons. On April 28 thousands of people from Southall again took to the streets to march, silently, in memory of Peach and raise defiant clenched fists at the spot where he was struck down. Later, in June, more than 8,000 people attended an all-night vigil at the Dominion Cinema, where his body lay in state, to pray and pay their last respects to him on the eve of his funeral. Thousands of pounds were collected in local shops, factories, homes and temples to send to the Blair Peach Memorial Fund, set up by colleagues and friends in the East End for his widow and children.

The events of April 23 and the death of Blair Peach were to reverberate both within Southall and beyond. The inquest and the Home Secretary's refusal to order an official inquiry, the trials of the Asian youth, and the revelations of the role of the Special Patrol Group on that day met with a nationwide response, echoing in different ways deep-seated anger at the police in many different parts of the country.

'Death by misadventure'

Even before the inquest on Peach's death started, the Director of Public Prosecutions announced, on the basis of the internal police investigation, that no policeman was to be prosecuted. The inquest itself was adjourned because the coroner turned down a request for a jury hearing of the evidence. In November the High Court, presided over by the Lord Chief Justice, Lord Widgery, turned down the defence application for a jury. One of the judges, Griffiths, stated that: 'On its worst construction, this is one isolated occasion of a policeman possibly using a weapon he should not have used, and hitting too hard.' This decision was overturned by the Court of Appeal just before Christmas, after press exposures of the weapons found in the lockers of members of the Special Patrol Group.

Despite this rebuke the coroner played a major role in determining the jury's findings. Despite months of police investigation no one officer could be brought forward as the perpetrator. Yet the jury heard of weapons (termed 'souvenirs' by the police) found in the SPG officers' lockers, including one leather-encased metal truncheon with knotted thong, two sledge-hammer handles, one rhino whip, one knife with a six-inch blade, two three-foot crowbars and a stave of wood three-foot long. More than a year after Peach's death the jury, on the firm advice of the coroner, brought in a verdict of 'death by misadventure'. However, they added three riders to this, including the recommendations that there should be more control of the SPG by its officers and that no unauthorised weapons or implements should be available in police stations.

The death of Blair Peach could not be completely brushed under the carpet, despite the verdict of the inquest. Initially, Metropolitan Police Commissioner Sir David McNee tried to dismiss criticisms of the SPG with comments like: 'If you keep off the streets of London and behave yourselves, you won't have the SPG to worry about' (said to a black journalist when presenting his annual report in June). But increasingly, throughout the rest of 1979 and during 1980, he and the Home Secretary William Whitelaw were forced to defend the existence of the SPG. Recruitment to the SPG was halted for nine months; a 'review' was carried out, which aimed at creating the impression of major changes. In fact, it was a cosmetic exercise in public relations, resulting only in limiting the length of service within the SPG to four years and decentralising its command structure – neither of which addressed the basic criticisms of its role and practice. After the search of the SPG lockers, three constables and an inspector were just transferred out of the SPG.

Ironically, the government's refusal to hold an inquiry, along the lines of that held on the death of Kevin Gately in Red Lion Square in 1974, acted as a public focus for looking at police activities. Reports on Southall were produced by Southall Rights, the National Council for Civil Liberties, the Runnymede Trust and the Commission for Racial Equality – all condemned the police action on April 23 and the handling of the subsequent trials. Outside Southall, the 'saturation policing' raids by the SPG in London – in Lambeth, Lewisham, Hackney and Brent – and elsewhere were attacked by local community leaders. All called for the disbandment of the SPG. Lewisham Council threatened to withhold its police rate unless the London police were made more accountable to the local community, while Lambeth Council set up an 18-month long inquiry into police-community relations.

Other events – the death of Jimmy Kelly in Merseyside, the use of 'sus' against young black people, deaths in custody and the Bristol 'riot' against the police – led to demands for greater police accountability.

The events of April 23 and the aftermath ensured that Blair Peach did not die in vain, and will not be forgotten.

The trials

Immediately after April 23 preparations had to be made in Southall to form a defence committee for those arrested. 342 people, mostly Asian and local, were charged with offences – the largest number in a single day since the CND mass sit-downs in the early 1960s. The charges ranged from assault or obstruction to the possession of offensive weapons. The handling of the charges and the trials mirrored the police response on the streets. Charges were changed so that only a handful could opt for trial by jury, and it was decided to hear nearly all the cases not in Southall but in Barnet, 25 miles away.

The fact of the trials brought the community together, but the circumstances made the job of the defence committee incredibly difficult. Money was collected, bulletins were produced on the progress of the cases, defendants were advised and public meetings were addressed up and down the country to draw attention to what was happening. But the tactic of moving the hearings to Barnet not only made it difficult for defendants and witnesses to get to court, but crucially removed them from the community and the potential mass support that would have been given in the courtroom and outside.

What compounded this tactic was the attitude of the magistrates hearing the cases. However contradictory or implausible the police evidence, it was generally accepted by the magistrates without question, even when faced with convincing evidence from defence witnesses. Removed from the community and the public eye, the magistrates handed out convictions in over 80 per cent of cases for weeks on end. Eventually, by enlisting the help of sympathetic lawyers and journalists and attracting enough publicity, the conviction rate dropped to 50 per cent in the remaining weeks of the trials. But for most it was already too late.

The most notorious example of the unquestioning acceptance of police evidence was the case of a juvenile who was said by the sole prosecution witness, a policeman, to have been running down Southall Broadway holding a brick in his bandaged hand. The magistrates heard evidence from a doctor, a lawyer, an ambulanceman and four other witnesses that the boy was having his hand bandaged in the Peoples Unite headquarters when he was arrested, and that his hand was so tightly bandaged that he would not have been able to hold anything. In spite of this evidence, he was convicted, and, to add insult to injury, was told to get a job (at 14!) to pay the fine. On at least two occasions defence witnesses, not charged with any offences themselves, were treated as criminals and bound over to keep the peace.

Whatever faith the community had in British justice was wiped out by these trials. The people had seen enough to feel that what they were getting was colonial justice – justice that served only to keep them in their place.

Living with the aftermath

For the black community in Southall life will never be the same again. April 23 was the culmination of a history of struggle and, at the same time, the beginning of a new stage of community action and resistance – in employment, education, housing, health care and dealings with the police.

In the Autumn of 1979 Southall IWA met with other black and anti-racist groups to form a national Campaign Against Racist Laws. Southall Black Sisters was also formed, to fight racism particularly as it affects black women. In March 1980 20 women were ejected by police from Ealing Town Hall after disrupting a Housing Committee meeting for failing to provide for the homeless. In June 1980 Southall Community Action was set up to campaign for better facilities in the area. In the same month, the IWA and EHAS demanded a review of Ealing's housing policy on the grounds that it was racially discriminatory. Indeed, discrimination by the local council has become more blatant. Councillor Wood, Ealing's spokesperson on housing, stated on television in November 1980 that: 'People in Southall will either have to put up with poor conditions ... or they will have to move elsewhere.'

Over the past two years racial attacks have continued unabated and confidence in the police – both in their treatment of such incidents and the protection they afford the black community – is at an all-time low. The local police chief, Chief Superintendent Dee, told *Police Review* in November 1980 that racial attacks 'are decreasing' and that 'There hasn't been a single public disturbance here since April 1979.' The reality is very different. During November 1979 alone, a gang of 50 skinheads threw bottles, bricks and knives into a pub full of Asians; another white gang threw milk bottles at an Asian motorist, yelling 'Pakis go home'; and two Asian families refused to send their children to school because they were being terrorised by white pupils and the police would not assist. In May 1980 an Asian waiting for a bus was pushed into the path of a passing car by a skinhead, and in July two Asian men were chased out of a 'white' pub and attacked outside. These instances are but a few of the flood of reports and calls for help recorded by Southall Rights and other organisations.

In July 1980 Mahmoud Mughal was attacked by 12 white youths on his way home. He was kicked and beaten and left lying on the pavement. Derek Gosse, the police Community Liaison Officer said: 'We do not believe it's a racial attack.' Following this, representatives of the Temples, the Mosques and the Southall Youth Movement met the police to demand greater protection from racist attacks. The meeting failed to produce any such commitment from the police. On August 3, 1980, the group met to launch a campaign, SCARA (Southall Campaign Against Racist Attacks). A committee was set up to represent the black community and to monitor racial attacks and police harassment.*

The attacks continued unabated, however, and the police response took the form, more and more, of attacking critics, denying the element of racism in the attacks, and sometimes denying the attacks themselves and turning on the victims.

On July 3, 1981, three coachloads of young skinheads from the East End came into Southall for a concert at the notorious Hambrough Tavern. On the way to the pub the skinheads terrorised Asian shopkeepers and shoppers, smashed shop windows, shouted racial abuse and attacked one Asian woman. As in 1976, news of the invasion spread rapidly and within an hour several hundred local youths – mostly Asian, but with a fair number of West Indians and some white youths – gathered at the Hambrough to do battle with the skinheads and send them packing. Police arrived to protect the skinheads from the anger of the town's youth. The evening ended with the Hambrough burnt out, many police injured – and the skinheads gone. The following day, the youths justified their action to the national media. 'If the police will not protect our community, we have to defend ourselves'. In Southall itself the explanation was not needed; it was self-evident. The community's response to the night's events was overwhelmingly supportive of the youth; overwhelmingly relieved that at last the racist attackers had been confronted and beaten off decisively.

There will be new groupings, new forms of struggle in Southall. But the past struggles – those we have documented here – have been the constant expression of a community's ability to take the experiences of exploitation, of neglect, of hostility and hatred –

*The body of this pamphlet was completed in November 1980.

and from them build strength, determination, resistance. The events of April 23, 1979, showed that a black community had indeed been born.

Bibliography

The following material has been drawn upon in the compilation of this pamphlet.

Books

Abbott, Simon (ed.), *The Prevention of Racial Discrimination in Britain*, 1971
Aurora, G.S., *The New Frontiersmen*, 1967
Bidwell, Sidney, *Red, White and Black*, 1976
Deakin, Nicholas (ed.), *Colour and the British Electorate 1964*, 1965
Foot, Paul, *Immigration and Race Relations in British Politics*, 1965
Hill, Michael, and Issacharoff, Ruth, *Community Action and Race Relations*, 1971
Hiro, Dilip, *Black British, White British*, 1973
John, Dewitt, *Indian Workers' Associations in Britain*, 1969
Marsh, Peter, *The Anatomy of a Strike*, 1967
Patterson, Sheila, *Immigrants and Race Relations in Britain 1960-67*, 1969
Walker, Martin, *The National Front*, 1977

Pamphlets

Counter Information Services/Institute of Race Relations, *Racism Who Profits?*, 1976
Ealing Community Relations Council, *School and Community in a Multi-cultural Area*, nd
Ealing International Friendship Committee, *The Education of the Immigrant Child in the London Borough of Ealing*, 1968
Indian Workers' Association, *Children In Southall*, 1969
'Joint Reports and Submissions of the Overseas and European Divisions of the Catering Units of the British Airways Corporation to the Race Relations Board', 1975
Kogan, Maurice, *Dispersal in the Ealing Local Education Authority Schools System*, 1975
National Council for Civil Liberties, *The Death of Blair Peach*, 1980
National Council for Civil Liberties, *Southall 23 April 1979*, 1980
Pullé, Stanislaus, *Police Immigrant Relations in Southall*, 1973

Ransom, David *License to Kill: the Blair Peach case,* 1980
Sandhu, Resham, *Race, Class and Political Action*, 1977
Sivanandan, A., *Race, Class and the State,* 1976
Southall Rights, *A Report on the events of 23rd April 1979,* 1980
Southall Socialist Workers Party, *Southall: the fight for our future,* 1979
West London Communist Party, *Bussing*, nd.

Reports, documents, minutes, newsletters of:
Clean Up Southall Campaign
Ealing Community Relations Council (formerly Ealing International Friendship Committee)
Ealing Environment Project
Ealing Housing Action Area Project
Ealing Housing Aid Service
Indian Workers' Association, Southall
London Borough of Ealing
National Association of Asian Youth
Southall Action Group
Southall Campaign Against Racist Attacks
Southall Rights

Periodicals and papers
The Asian
Des Perdes
Ealing Gazette
Institute of Race Relations *Newsletter*
LAG Bulletin
Middlesex County Times
New Community
New Society
New Statesman
Punjab Times
Race & Class (formerly *Race*)
Race Today
Sandesh
Southall Gazette
Time Out
and the national press

Calendar

1951

333 Commonwealth immigrants in Ealing (pop. 55,896).

1957

IWA (Southall) formed.

1958

1,250 Asians, 150 Jamaicans in Ealing.

1959

Gurdwara founded in Southall.

1961

IWA opposes Commonwealth Immigrants Bill.

1962

Commonwealth Immigrants Act passed. Southall's Labour MP, George Pargiter, votes against it.

1963

TGWU branch set up in Woolf's.
BNP wins large share of vote in local elections.
Southall Residents' Association formed.
Southall International Friendship Committee formed.

1964

General Election: Pargiter changes position on immigration.

1965

Southall incorporated into new London Borough of Ealing.
White Paper on immigration.
IWA affiliates to CARD (Campaign Against Racial Discrimination).
Black people form 11% of Ealing's population.
Attempt by local Tories and some Labour to bring in 15-year residence qualification for blacks to get council housing.
Woolf's strike; Rockware Glass strike.

1966

General Election: BNP stand.
Outbreak of racist attacks.
BNP merges with Tyndall's Greater Britain Movement.
Strike at Chibnall's Bakery.
Indian National Association campaign to tidy the town.
First black family gets council housing in Southall.

1967

First black councillor elected.
NF stand in Ealing local elections.
IWA buys Dominion Cinema.
JCWI (Joint Council for the Welfare of Immigrants) formed by IWA and others.
TGWU Greenford calls for ban on immigration, opposed by Ealing Trades Council.

1968

Powell's 'Rivers of Blood' speech.
AEC workers march for Powell; branches of other unions call for ban on immigration. Southall TGWU declares itself against racialism.
Racial attacks on Asians at school.
IWA march against Commonwealth Immigrants Act.
SRA candidates win local seats in Northcote and Glebe wards.

1969

NF, SRA, RPS (Racial Preservation Society) march through Southall.
IWA campaign on bussing and lack of play groups.

1970

RPS literature circulated in Southall.
NF stands in General Election.
West Indian youth shot in racial incident.
Ealing CRC demands urgent improvements in housing for Southall, calls for more schools in Southall to end bussing.

1971

Council attacks Ealing CRC for 'political propaganda' on housing; cuts its grant.
Campaign to end bussing continues (through to 1975).
IWA starts Saturday school and summer schools.
Immigration Act.
Powell speaks at Southall Chamber of Commerce.
Caribbean Overseas Association (Acton) burned down in third fire in a fortnight.

1972

Ugandan Asians 'scare'; Bidwell says no more for Southall.

1973

Protests at Southall police brutality and treatment of suspected illegal immigrants.
IWA breaks with Ealing CRC in protest at retrospective application of Immigration Act.
Perivale-Gutterman strike and lock-out.
Strike at Lyons, Greenford.

1974

Perivale-Gutterman strike ends.
General Election; no NF candidate in Southall.
Ealing CRO blames bussing for bullying of Asian children at school.
IWA and Afro-Caribbean Association protest against racism in local schools.
Pullé report on police-immigrant relations condemns police.
Black student killed on way to school by whites.

1975

Official report on bussing says it 'may be discriminatory'.
Southall Campaign Against Racism formed.

1976

Gurdip Singh Chaggar killed; Southall Youth Movement formed.
Local groups demonstrate at Heathrow against racist immigration procedures.
Strikes at British Airways catering, Dura Tube Wires, Chibnall Bakeries.

1977

Black bookshop in Ealing, Ealing CRC and Southall progressive bookshop suffer series of attacks — paint, slogans, KKK stickers.

1978

Ealing Council goes Tory.
Attempt to let hall to NF abandoned after noisy protests.
Peoples Unite started around reggae group Misty. Rock Against Racism Carnival.
Many complaints of police harassment, particularly towards black youth.

1979

Council bans open-air concerts.
Peoples Unite premises raided by police; station picketed.
Council refuses to ban St Georges Day meeting at Southall Town Hall.
April 23 — 700 arrested, 342 charged, one killed, hundreds injured in police operation to clear Southall for NF meeting.
All contents of Peoples Unite building destroyed or damaged by police.

1979

April
10,000 march in Southall to mourn death of Blair Peach.

May
Peoples Unite building bulldozed to ground by Council two weeks after April 23 — two years ahead of schedule.
AEC Southall closes; 2,500 jobs lost.
Tories win General Election.

June
2,000 participate in national black people's march against state brutality.
Search of SPG lockers reveals lethal weapons; 4 officers transferred as disciplinary measure.
8,000 Southall people mourn Peach in all-night vigil.
Thousands march in East London at Peach's funeral.

July
Picket marks start of 'Southall 342' trials at Barnet.
Leaked CRE report on April 23 alleges gross police brutality.

August
44-year-old S.S. Grewal dies in Southall Police Station.

October
Pickets of police stations on eve of Peach inquest demand disbandment of SPG, end to Southall trials.
Ealing Council announces proposals to cut nearly £2½m from housing, education, social services budget.

November
Firestone (Brentford) closes; 1,500 jobs lost.
Campaign Against Racist Laws set up with IWA Southall.
Southall Black Sisters formed.
Racist attacks by gangs of skinheads in Southall.
Lawyers representing 'Southall 342' petition Lord Chancellor on injustice of trials.
March through London against trials, racist laws.

1980

January
Mass picket at Chix (Slough) where Asian women, many from Southall, on strike.

February
Ealing Council announces plans to sell multi-racial school to Church of England.

March
Protests in Southall about projected lorry park, lack of provision for homeless.
Sikh Temple bids to buy High School in Southall, saying British educational system failing their children.

April
New Punjabi newspaper launched in Southall.
Runnymede Trust report on Southall trials reveals gross miscarriages of justice.
Tory councillor calls pro-SPG march through Ealing for April 23.
National pickets of police stations on 1st anniversary of April 23, 1979.
NCCL report condemns police operation as disastrous and brutal.

May
Perivale Maternity Hospital reprieved from closure after campaign to save it.
Explosion destroys Indian-owned launderette in Southall, treated as arson.
Peach inquest jury returns verdict of misadventure.

June
British Leyland cuts 650 jobs at Park Royal factory.
Southall Community Action set up to fight for better local facilities.
IWA Southall and Ealing Housing Aid urge review of Ealing's 'racially discriminatory' housing policy.
Chix strike ends.
Northfields Labour Party withholds part of rates as protest at non-accountability of police.

July
35 jobs lost at Crown Cork, Southall.
Asians on Northolt estate ask Ealing Council for protection against skinhead gangs.

August
SCARA (Southall Campaign Against Racist Attacks) set up after vast increase in attacks to monitor police action; Southall police deny racial violence on increase.
Dilloway (Southall) closes, 23 jobs lost; 99 jobs lost at Lyons Greenford; 53 going at Quaker (Southall).
Report shows unemployment in Southall has risen 54% in year; 36% for men, 88% for women.

October
Forged letter tells Ealing householders that 70% of new housing estate reserved for blacks.
Two-week protest campaign by local groups at Ealing's housing policies in Southall.
Skinhead attack on 4-year-old with boiling wax and paint; police take no action.
Ealing black bookshop daubed with racist slogans.

November
Ealing's housing spokesman tells Southall people to get out of the Borough if they want decent housing.